Welcome to the **World Explorer's Quiz Book**, where curiosity meets adventure! Whether you're a seasoned traveler or someone who dreams of exploring far-off lands from the comfort of your couch, this book is designed to challenge your knowledge and ignite your sense of wonder. Inside, you'll find questions that dive deep into geography, culture, history, and those quirky little facts that make every corner of the world unique.

This isn't your average quiz book. It's a journey—one that will take you from the bustling streets of Tokyo to the ancient ruins of Rome, from the fjords of Norway to the deserts of Namibia. Along the way, you'll encounter riddles, puzzles, and clues that will test not just what you know, but how you think about the world around you. Ready to see how much of a world explorer you really are? Let's dive in!

Contents

Quiz 1

World Leaders: Who Am I?

Welcome to the **"World Leaders: Who Am I?"** quiz, where politics meets personality! Think you know your heads of state and global power players? It's time to put your geopolitical savvy to the test! In this quiz, you'll encounter cryptic, witty clues that hint at the movers and shakers shaping our world today. But beware, it's not all straightforward—expect some tongue-in-cheek references, quirky details, and clues that demand a bit of creative thinking. From mighty presidents and fierce prime ministers to kings in all but name, these leaders are at the helm of the nations that make the headlines.

Ready to solve these diplomatic riddles? Let's begin!

1. I'm often seen riding high through vast lands, shirtless, some might say. My icy stare could freeze time, and I've held power longer than most of my peers. My recent moves in Eastern Europe have kept the world on edge.
   ### Who am I?
2. With golden locks and quick quips, I led a famous capital through a pandemic, and I'm often compared to a certain teddy bear of a U.S.

president. I left the stage, but not without a stir. I've always had a flair for the dramatic.

Who am I?

3. A man with a name that sounds like an artist, but my creations are laws and policies in a vast democracy. I love chai and yoga, and I've become a strong symbol of my nation's return to its roots, though not without stirring controversy.

Who am I?

4. The weight of my nation's economic superpower rests on my shoulders. I'm seen as calm, calculating, and a builder of bridges—literally and diplomatically. Though the Great Wall is centuries old, my country is still growing stronger.

Who am I?

5. I'm a former comedian turned fierce wartime leader. You might recognize my green t-shirt more than my suit these days, as I navigate an ongoing struggle with a large neighbor. My speeches have inspired the free world to stand with me.

Who am I?

6. I'm an island queen, but I don't wear a crown. While many thought my rule would end, I managed to keep the waves from crashing. Known for my sharp words and quiet resolve, I

led my island nation out of a long union and into new, stormy seas.

Who am I?

7. A historic first in my continent, I represent change, unity, and progress. Leading a nation known for diamonds and Mandela, my role as a leader is about far more than policy. My presence is a beacon for equality and hope.

Who am I?

8. A "prince" among leaders, I've played the long game in a kingdom rich with oil and tradition. While reforms have shocked some, others praise me for loosening the royal reins. I've had to navigate both praise and criticism for my bold moves on the global stage.

Who am I?

9. My country is famous for tulips and bicycles, but my tenure was long and steady, more like a windmill's slow turn. Some have called me "Teflon," as crises slid off me, yet I stepped down after many years at the helm of Europe's core power.

Who am I?

10. I'm both warrior and king, though my kingdom doesn't wear a crown. My national emblem is the eagle, and while my homeland's age is young compared to others, my impact

echoes around the globe. Some say I build walls, but I see them as bridges.

Who am I?

Answers

1. Vladimir Putin – President of Russia

- Putin is a former KGB officer and has been either President or Prime Minister of Russia since 1999, making him one of the longest-serving leaders in modern times. His shirtless photos during outdoor activities are often seen as part of his strongman persona. Recently, his controversial invasion of Ukraine has intensified geopolitical tensions, referencing the "icy stare" and "moves in Eastern Europe."

2. Boris Johnson – Former Prime Minister of the United Kingdom

- Known for his unruly blonde hair and eccentric personality, Boris Johnson was Mayor of London before becoming Prime Minister in 2019. His leadership during Brexit and the COVID-19 pandemic earned him both praise and criticism. The reference to the "teddy bear" refers to comparisons with Teddy Roosevelt due to their shared flamboyant leadership styles.

3. Narendra Modi – Prime Minister of India

- Modi, in power since 2014, is known for his promotion of Hindu nationalism and economic reforms. He has promoted yoga globally and enjoys simple pleasures like chai (Indian tea). Modi's administration has been polarizing, with both support for his development initiatives and criticism over religious and minority policies.

4. Xi Jinping – President of China

- Xi Jinping has led China since 2012 and is the architect of China's massive Belt and Road Initiative, which aims to strengthen infrastructure and trade links around the world. His leadership has seen China rise as a superpower, though his presidency has also been marked by crackdowns on dissent and increasing authoritarianism.

5. Volodymyr Zelenskyy – President of Ukraine

- Zelenskyy rose to fame as an actor and comedian before becoming Ukraine's president in 2019. He played a fictional president on TV before being elected in real life. Since the Russian invasion of Ukraine in 2022, he has become an international symbol of resistance, often seen in military fatigues as he leads his country in wartime.

6. Theresa May – Former Prime Minister of the United Kingdom

- May led the UK through the difficult and tumultuous Brexit negotiations, serving as Prime Minister from 2016 to 2019. Though she faced criticism and ultimately resigned, she was known for her quiet determination and sharp negotiation skills. Her nickname "Maybot" references her often stoic public demeanor.

7. Cyril Ramaphosa – President of South Africa

- Ramaphosa, a former anti-apartheid activist, trade union leader, and businessman, became South Africa's president in 2018. He succeeded Jacob Zuma and is often seen as a steady, unifying force. His leadership focuses on economic reform, anti-corruption, and national unity. The reference to "diamonds" ties to South Africa's natural resources.

8. Mohammed bin Salman (MBS) – Crown Prince of Saudi Arabia

- MBS has been the de facto ruler of Saudi Arabia since 2017, driving major social and economic reforms, including allowing women to drive and curbing the influence of the religious police. However, his rule has been controversial, especially due to the murder of journalist Jamal

Khashoggi, for which international pressure has mounted.

9. Mark Rutte – Former Prime Minister of the Netherlands

- Rutte was one of Europe's longest-serving leaders, serving as Prime Minister of the Netherlands from 2010 to 2023. He's known for his calm, pragmatic approach to leadership, often navigating crises with a steady hand. He was referred to as "Teflon Mark" for his ability to emerge from political scandals relatively unscathed.

10. Joe Biden – President of the United States

- Biden, inaugurated in 2021, is the oldest U.S. president to take office. His presidency has focused on repairing international relations, tackling climate change, and addressing domestic issues like the pandemic. The reference to "warrior" ties to his long political career, and the "king" is a nod to his position at the helm of the world's most powerful democracy. His stance on immigration and building border walls has been a key talking point.

Quiz 2

Culinary World Tour - Guess the Dish

Match each dish to the correct country. Use the cryptic hints to help you identify where these iconic foods are from.

Choose from the countries listed below

Easy Level (1-10)

- A. Italy
- B. Japan
- C. India
- D. Mexico
- E. France
- F. Greece
- G. Thailand
- H. Spain
- I. China
- J. Lebanon

1. This dish is often raw, wrapped in seaweed, and served with wasabi.

- It's an island nation famous for ancient warriors and cherry blossoms.

2. A street food staple, these small round flatbreads can be filled with spiced meat, salsa, and a squeeze of lime.

- This country's flag features green, white, and red, and it's known for its vibrant festivals.

3. A tangy, spicy dish that blends coconut milk, lemongrass, and chili paste, often served with rice.

- Famous for beautiful beaches and temples, this country is known for its bustling street food scene.

4. A rice-based dish cooked with saffron and seafood, often served in a shallow pan.

- Think Mediterranean – a place where flamenco and siestas are part of daily life.

5. A soft cheese-filled pastry that pairs perfectly with coffee, typically found in cozy cafés along the Seine.

- A country synonymous with romance, art, and the Eiffel Tower.

6. This popular dish is cooked in a tandoor oven and seasoned with yogurt and spices, creating a smoky, flavorful meal.

- The birthplace of Bollywood and home to the Taj Mahal.

7. Layers of pasta, cheese, and rich tomato sauce baked together to perfection.

- This country's cuisine is famous for pasta, wine, and olive oil, and is shaped like a boot.

8. A dish made with chickpeas, garlic, and sesame paste, often eaten with pita bread.

- A Middle Eastern country known for its ancient history and cedar trees.

9. A warm soup made with dumplings, usually served alongside tea.

- Known for the Great Wall and a rich culinary tradition dating back thousands of years.

10. This layered dish includes lamb, eggplant, and béchamel sauce, baked until golden.

- A country known for its mythological gods and famous ancient ruins.

Medium Level (11–20)

Countries:

A. Egypt
B. Belgium
C. Scotland
D. Brazil
E. Argentina
F. South Korea

G. Russia

H. Ethiopia

I. Turkey

J. Germany

11. French Fries

- Despite the name, these crispy fried potatoes are often linked with this small European country famous for chocolate and waffles.

12. Chicken Tikka Masala

- Often mistaken for an Indian dish, this spiced, creamy chicken dish was created in this country, which is also home to haggis and bagpipes.

13. Kimchi

- A fermented cabbage dish packed with spice and probiotics, this dish comes from a country known for K-pop, technological innovation, and rich food traditions.

14. Döner Kebab

- This savory, slow-roasted meat dish is served in flatbread with vegetables and sauces. It's a favorite street food in a country that bridges Europe and Asia.

15. Chimichurri Steak

- A green sauce made from parsley, garlic, and vinegar is drizzled over grilled beef in a country where gauchos and tango dance are part of the culture.

16. Koshari

- This hearty dish mixes rice, lentils, and pasta, topped with spicy tomato sauce and crispy onions, and comes from a country with one of the Seven Wonders of the Ancient World.

17. Pelmeni

- These dumplings are filled with meat and sometimes served in broth, originating from a country known for its cold winters, vodka, and vast history.

18. Bratwurst

- A traditional sausage often served with mustard, this food comes from a country known for its beer, festivals, and automotive industry.

19. Feijoada

- A black bean stew made with pork, typically enjoyed during large family gatherings in a South American country famous for carnival and samba.

20. Injera with Wat

- This spongy flatbread is used to scoop up a spicy, slow-cooked stew in a country known for its ancient Christian churches and unique coffee ceremony.

Hard Level (21–30)

Countries:

A. Malaysia

B. Peru

C. Iceland

D. Vietnam

E. Finland

F. Sweden

G. Denmark

H. Morocco

I. Nigeria

J. Norway

21. Tagine

- This slow-cooked stew of meat and vegetables, often flavored with saffron, cumin, and preserved lemons, is cooked in a cone-shaped pot. It hails from a North African country known for its desert landscapes and colorful markets.

22. Surströmming

- Known as one of the world's smelliest foods, this fermented fish is a delicacy in a Scandinavian country known for its archipelagos and minimalist design.

23. Ceviche

- A dish of raw fish marinated in citrus juices, usually served with corn and sweet potato, from a South American country famous for the Andes and ancient Incan cities.

24. Karjalanpiirakka

- A rye pastry filled with rice porridge, traditionally eaten with butter, in a country known for its thousands of lakes and love of saunas.

25. Smørrebrød

- An open-faced sandwich topped with ingredients like herring, eggs, and liver pate, served in a country known for its Viking history and cycling culture.

26. Rakfisk

- A dish of fermented fish, often trout, served raw. This delicacy comes from a country famous for its fjords and Viking heritage.

27. Nasi Lemak

- A dish consisting of coconut rice, sambal, anchovies, and boiled eggs, wrapped in banana leaves, from a Southeast Asian country with a diverse culinary heritage.

28. Jollof Rice

- A one-pot dish made from tomatoes, onions, and spices, served in a West African country with vibrant cultures, oil wealth, and Nollywood.

29. Hákarl

- A fermented shark dish that is often left to rot for several months before being consumed in a country famous for its glaciers and volcanic landscapes.

30. Pho

- A noodle soup made with fragrant broth, fresh herbs, and thinly sliced beef or chicken, hailing from a Southeast Asian country with a long history of street food and French colonial influence.

Answers: Culinary World Tour

Guess the Dish

Easy

1. B. Japan – Sushi

- Sushi originated as a way to preserve fish in fermented rice during ancient Japan. Today, it's a highly regarded cuisine, with sushi chefs undergoing years of training.

2. D. Mexico – Tacos

- Tacos have been eaten since the times of the ancient Aztecs. They are usually filled with various ingredients like carnitas, barbacoa, or even grasshoppers!

3. G. Thailand – Pad Thai

- Pad Thai became popular in Thailand during World War II when the government promoted it as a national dish to reduce rice consumption.

4. H. Spain – Paella

- Paella originated in the Valencia region of Spain. Traditional versions of the dish can include not only seafood but also rabbit and chicken.

5. E. France – Croissant

- Although now a French staple, the croissant was inspired by Austrian pastries. The French adapted the recipe to create the buttery, flaky version we enjoy today.

6. C. India – Butter Chicken

- Butter Chicken, or "Murgh Makhani," was invented in Delhi in the 1950s. It's often paired with naan or basmati rice and has become a global favorite.

7. Italy – Lasagna

- Lasagna is one of the oldest known types of pasta, dating back to the Roman Empire. Regional variations across Italy may include béchamel sauce or ricotta cheese.

8. Lebanon – Hummus

- Hummus is a popular dish in the Middle East, but Lebanon is known for its particularly rich and creamy version. It's often served as part of a mezze platter.

9. China – Dim Sum

- Dim Sum, meaning "touch the heart," consists of bite-sized dishes traditionally served with tea. The Cantonese are famous for their dim sum culture.

10. F. Greece – Moussaka

- Moussaka is a classic dish in Greek cuisine, but its roots may stretch back to the Arab world. The modern version was popularized by a Greek chef in the 1920s.

Medium

11. B. Belgium – French Fries

- Despite being called "French" fries, this dish likely originated in Belgium, where villagers fried potatoes in the 17th century. The confusion arises from American soldiers in World War I who ate fries prepared by French-speaking Belgian soldiers.

12. C. Scotland – Chicken Tikka Masala

- Chicken Tikka Masala was reportedly created in a Glasgow restaurant in the 1970s. The chef added a tomato cream sauce to grilled chicken at a customer's request, creating this now-iconic dish.

13. F. South Korea – Kimchi

- Kimchi, a fermented vegetable dish, has been a part of Korean cuisine for thousands of years. There are over 200 types of kimchi, and it's often served at every meal in Korea.

14. I. Turkey – Döner Kebab

- The döner kebab originated in Turkey in the 19th century and has since spread across the world, especially in Europe, where it's a popular late-night snack.

15. E. Argentina – Chimichurri Steak

- Chimichurri is a green sauce made of parsley, garlic, and vinegar, typically served over grilled meats in Argentina, one of the world's largest beef producers.

16. A. Egypt – Koshari

- Koshari is considered Egypt's national dish and is a hearty meal often sold at street stalls. It's a combination of leftover pantry items like rice, lentils, and pasta, making it a symbol of resourcefulness.

17. G. Russia – Pelmeni

- Pelmeni, a type of dumpling filled with minced meat, is often eaten during Russian winters. The dumplings are sometimes frozen outdoors in Siberia, where temperatures can drop extremely low.

18. J. Germany – Bratwurst

- Bratwurst is a type of German sausage made from pork, beef, or veal. It's typically grilled or fried and served with mustard and sauerkraut. Germany is known for its wide variety of sausages.

19. D. Brazil – Feijoada

- Feijoada, a black bean and pork stew, is Brazil's national dish. It's typically eaten on Wednesdays and Saturdays and is believed to have been created by enslaved people using leftover pork parts.

20. H. Ethiopia – Injera with Wat

- Injera is a spongy flatbread made from teff flour, used to scoop up dishes like "wat" (stew) in Ethiopia. It also serves as a plate, with diners breaking off pieces to scoop up their food.

Hard

21. H. Morocco – Tagine

- The tagine is both the name of the dish and the earthenware pot it's cooked in. The slow-cooking method allows the flavors of the spices like saffron and cumin to develop fully.

22. F. Sweden – Surströmming

- Surströmming, fermented Baltic herring, is notorious for its pungent smell. In Sweden, it's traditionally eaten outdoors with flatbread and potatoes to lessen the smell.

23. B. Peru – Ceviche

- Ceviche is Peru's national dish and has been consumed for over 2,000 years. The citric acid in lime "cooks" the fish, which is why no heat is required.

24. E. Finland – Karjalanpiirakka

- Karjalanpiirakka is a traditional Finnish pastry from the region of Karelia. It's often served with egg butter and eaten at family gatherings or holidays.

25. G. Denmark – Smørrebrød

- Smørrebrød, meaning "butter bread," is an open-faced sandwich. Toppings vary widely, but popular choices include fish, eggs, and cold cuts.

26. J. Norway – Rakfisk

- Rakfisk is a traditional Norwegian dish of fermented fish, typically trout. The fermentation process can take up to a year, and it's usually eaten during Christmas.

27. A. Malaysia – Nasi Lemak

- Nasi Lemak is considered Malaysia's national dish and is often eaten for breakfast. The fragrant rice is cooked in coconut milk, and the dish is wrapped in banana leaves for extra flavor.

28. I. Nigeria – Jollof Rice

- Jollof rice is a West African favorite, and it has sparked a friendly rivalry between Nigeria and Ghana over whose version is best. It's often served at celebrations and gatherings.

29. C. Iceland – Hákarl

- Hákarl is fermented Greenland shark, a traditional Icelandic dish. The shark's meat is toxic when fresh, so it's buried in gravel for months to ferment, then dried before eating.

30. D. Vietnam – Pho

- Pho is a Vietnamese noodle soup that's become a global sensation. It's traditionally eaten as a breakfast dish in Vietnam and is made with beef or chicken, topped with fresh herbs.

Quiz 3

Famous Train Journeys - Choose Your Scenic Route!

Each question describes a famous train journey. Use the clues about the views, landmarks, and cultural elements you'll encounter to match the train to the correct country or countries. Select the right answer from the options below.

1. The Glacier Express

This is the slowest express train in the world, winding its way through snow-capped peaks, deep gorges, and picturesque alpine villages. The journey offers breathtaking views of a famous mountain and crosses over 291 bridges.

    A. Switzerland

    B. Austria

    C. Germany

    D. France

In this country, timepieces are as renowned as its peaks. You may want to yodel if you take this journey.

2. The Trans-Siberian Railway

Covering 9,289 kilometers, this legendary train ride is one of the longest in the world. It cuts through icy landscapes, birch forests, and endless steppes, passing mighty mountain ranges and the world's deepest freshwater lake.

A. Russia

B. Mongolia

C. China

D. Russia/Mongolia

Traversing a land where winters are long and the bear is the national symbol, this journey spans two continents.

3. The Rocky Mountaineer

This luxury train winds through rugged mountains, passing sparkling lakes, thick forests, and towering peaks. It travels through dramatic canyons and along the edge of deep rivers.

A. United States

B. Canada

C. New Zealand

D. Alaska

Known for politeness and maple leaves, this country offers breathtaking scenery and a chance to spot a moose.

4. The Orient Express

Known as the setting for a famous mystery novel, this elegant journey passes through some of Europe's most historic and beautiful cities. Lavish dining cars and luxurious cabins are the hallmark of this iconic train.

A. United Kingdom
B. France/Italy
C. France/Turkey
D. Austria/Germany

This train journey takes you from the romance of baguettes to the allure of baklava, with a history as old as the Ottoman Empire.

5. The Blue Train

Known as one of the most luxurious train experiences, this train crosses scenic plains, stunning mountain ranges, and vast deserts. Along the way, you'll spot wildlife and visit colonial-era towns.

A. Kenya
B. South Africa
C. Egypt
D. Morocco

In the land where lions and elephants roam free, this train ride rivals safaris in splendor.

6. The Eastern & Oriental Express

This journey weaves through lush rainforests, ancient temples, and bustling tropical cities. You'll see rice paddies and rural villages, as well as colonial architecture and modern cityscapes.

A. Thailand/Malaysia
B. India
C. Singapore/Malaysia
D. Thailand/Singapore

From fragrant spices to tropical fruit, this journey links a paradise of islands with a city renowned for its futuristic skyline.

7. The Andean Explorer

As one of the highest train journeys in the world, this train takes you through stunning landscapes of high-altitude lakes, rugged mountains, and remote villages. The train passes through the heart of the Andes.

A. Peru
B. Chile
C. Argentina
D. Bolivia

Where ancient empires once thrived, you'll find soaring mountains, sacred valleys, and some pretty cute llamas.

8. The Ghan

This train crosses an entire continent, taking you from tropical coasts through the vast, arid outback and finally to a city known for its laid-back vibe. Along the way, you'll witness red deserts, rugged ranges, and vast wilderness.

    A. South Africa
    B. Australia
    C. Argentina
    D. United States

Named after camel riders from the Middle East, this journey traverses a continent where kangaroos hop and the Outback reigns supreme.

9. The Maharajas' Express

Known for its opulent interiors and royal treatment, this train journey passes through historical forts, palaces, and some of the most famous cultural landmarks in the world. Along the way, you'll witness deserts, bustling markets, and sacred rivers.

    A. India
    B. Pakistan
    C. Sri Lanka
    D. Bangladesh

Travel like royalty through a land of colors, spices, and centuries-old dynasties. This country is home to one of the world's most famous monuments of love.

10. The Bernina Express

This scenic train ride takes you through spectacular mountain landscapes, crossing the Alps and offering views of glaciers, lakes, and charming towns. It's famous for engineering marvels like the Landwasser Viaduct.

A. France/Italy
B. Austria/Switzerland
C. Germany/Switzerland
D. Switzerland/Italy

This journey connects the land of snow-capped peaks and precision watches with a country known for pizza, pasta, and artistic masterpieces.

Answers

1. A. Switzerland – The Glacier Express

- The Glacier Express connects two glamorous resorts, Zermatt and St. Moritz, passing through the Swiss Alps. It crosses 291 bridges and 91 tunnels, including the iconic Oberalp Pass at over 2,000 meters above sea level. You can also glimpse the Matterhorn on this unforgettable ride!

2. A. Russia – The Trans-Siberian Railway

- The Trans-Siberian Railway spans from Moscow to Vladivostok, a journey of nearly a week. Along the way, passengers cross the Ural Mountains, which divide Europe and Asia, and pass by Lake Baikal, the world's deepest and oldest freshwater lake. The railway has been crucial to connecting the vast expanses of Russia since its completion in 1916.

3. B. Canada – The Rocky Mountaineer

- The Rocky Mountaineer takes passengers through some of the most scenic parts of the Canadian Rockies, including Banff and Jasper National Parks. The train is renowned for its glass-domed carriages, allowing passengers to enjoy panoramic views of waterfalls, glaciers, and wildlife like bears and elk.

4. C. France/Turkey – The Orient Express

- The original Orient Express was launched in 1883 and became synonymous with luxury travel. Running from Paris to Istanbul, it passed through key European cities like Vienna, Budapest, and Sofia. Agatha Christie's novel *Murder on the Orient Express* added to the train's glamorous mystique.

5. B. South Africa – The Blue Train

- The Blue Train travels between Pretoria and Cape Town, offering a luxurious way to see South Africa's diverse landscapes. Along the way, passengers can see vast plains, dramatic mountains, and even wildlife, including antelope and zebras. The Blue Train has been a symbol of luxury since the 1920s.

6. D. Thailand/Singapore – The Eastern & Oriental Express

- The Eastern & Oriental Express is a luxurious journey through Southeast Asia, connecting Bangkok with Singapore. Passengers experience the beauty of Thailand's countryside, cross the famous River Kwai, and end their journey in Singapore's bustling cityscape. The train is famous for its art deco design and lavish onboard service.

7. A. Peru – The Andean Explorer

- The Andean Explorer travels through some of the highest terrain in the world, taking passengers from Cusco to Lake Titicaca and on to Arequipa. At its highest point, the train reaches over 4,800 meters above sea level, making it one of the highest train journeys in the world. The journey passes through the dramatic Peruvian Andes, home to ancient Incan history.

8. B. Australia – The Ghan

- The Ghan runs from Darwin in the north to Adelaide in the south, traversing nearly 3,000 kilometers through the Australian Outback. Named after Afghan cameleers who helped explore the interior of Australia, the train crosses stunning landscapes from tropical savannah to the red center of the country.

9. A. India – The Maharajas' Express

- The Maharajas' Express is often described as the "world's most luxurious train." It offers journeys through India's cultural heart, Rajasthan, with stops at historic forts, palaces, and temples. Passengers dine on gourmet meals while traveling in luxury, with views of India's diverse and vibrant landscapes.

10. D. Switzerland/Italy – The Bernina Express

- The Bernina Express travels between Switzerland and Italy, crossing the Swiss Alps and providing stunning views of glaciers, mountain passes, and alpine villages. It's famous for its engineering marvels, including the Landwasser Viaduct, a UNESCO World Heritage site. The journey connects the scenic beauty of Switzerland with the culture and cuisine of northern Italy.

Quiz 4

Airports and Airlines – True or False

1. The busiest airport in the world by passenger traffic is Dubai International Airport.
   True or False?
2. The airline known as "Qantas" is based in New Zealand.
   True or False?
3. Heathrow Airport is located in Paris, France.
   True or False?
4. Singapore Airlines is consistently ranked as one of the best airlines in the world.
   True or False?
5. JFK Airport in New York City is named after former U.S. President John F. Kennedy.
   True or False?
6. The longest commercial flight in the world is operated by Singapore Airlines from Singapore to New York.
   True or False?
7. Charles de Gaulle Airport is the largest airport in Italy.
   True or False?
8. Ryanair is known as a low-cost airline based in Ireland.

9. Hartsfield-Jackson Atlanta International Airport has held the title of the world's busiest airport for several years.

True or False?

10. The IATA code for Los Angeles International Airport is "LAX."

True or False?

11. Emirates is the national airline of Saudi Arabia.

True or False?

12. The airport with the longest runway in the world is in Bolivia.

True or False?

13. Lufthansa is the flag carrier airline of Germany.

True or False?

14. The world's first commercial flight took place in 1914.

True or False?

15. Narita Airport is located in Tokyo, Japan.

True or False?

Did you know? The world's largest airport by land area is King Fahd International Airport in Dammam, Saudi Arabia, covering a massive 780 square kilometers! While it's not the busiest, this airport is so large that it could fit multiple smaller airports inside its boundaries, and it even houses its own residential village. Despite its size, much of the land is undeveloped, making it a unique aviation hub.

Answer

1. **False** – The busiest airport by passenger traffic is Hartsfield-Jackson Atlanta International Airport, not Dubai International.
2. **False** – Qantas is the flag carrier airline of Australia, not New Zealand.
3. **False** – Heathrow Airport is located in London, England, not Paris.
4. **True** – Singapore Airlines is frequently ranked as one of the best airlines in the world for its service and comfort.
5. **True** – JFK Airport is indeed named after U.S. President John F. Kennedy.
6. **True** – Singapore Airlines operates the longest commercial flight from Singapore to New York.
7. **False** – Charles de Gaulle Airport is located in Paris, France, not Italy. The largest airport in Italy is Leonardo da Vinci–Fiumicino Airport in Rome.
8. **True** – Ryanair is a well-known low-cost airline based in Ireland.
9. **True** – Hartsfield-Jackson Atlanta International Airport has consistently been the world's busiest airport by passenger traffic.

10. **True** – The IATA code for Los Angeles International Airport is indeed "LAX."

11. **False** – Emirates is the national airline of the United Arab Emirates, not Saudi Arabia.

12. **True** – The longest commercial runway is located at El Alto International Airport in La Paz, Bolivia, due to its high altitude.

13. **True** – Lufthansa is the flag carrier airline of Germany.

14. **True** – The world's first commercial flight occurred in 1914 between St. Petersburg and Tampa, Florida.

15. **False** – Narita Airport is located near Tokyo, but it's actually in Narita, Chiba Prefecture, not within Tokyo itself.

Quiz 5

Film Locations Around the Globe
Volume 1

Each question gives you cryptic clues about the location of a famous movie. Match the movie to its filming location by using hints about the director, actors, and iconic scenes. Choose the correct answer from the options below.

1. In this eerie film directed by Stanley Kubrick, an isolated hotel provides the backdrop for one man's terrifying descent into madness. Jack Nicholson's chilling performance is unforgettable, but the actual location was filmed far from its supposed Colorado setting. A certain mountain range might give it away.

A. California, USA
B. Oregon, USA
C. British Columbia, Canada
D. Utah, USA

2. A sweeping romance with a deadly iceberg, directed by James Cameron. The lead actors, one an acclaimed actor from *The Revenant*, and the other an English Rose known for her role in *The Reader*, filmed a majority of this blockbuster not in the cold Atlantic but in a sunny coastal city.

A. Nova Scotia, Canada

B. Sydney, Australia

C. Rosarito, Mexico

D. Malta

3. In this Christopher Nolan thriller, reality and dreams blur as characters delve into subconscious heists. Starring Leonardo DiCaprio, the film's dream-like snow fortress sequence wasn't filmed in a far-flung dreamscape, but in this European ski resort.

A. Chamonix, France

B. Gstaad, Switzerland

C. Sölden, Austria

D. Cortina d'Ampezzo, Italy

4. This film about a young boy who lives in the Scottish Highlands was the directorial debut of Danny Boyle. Featuring stunning wilderness landscapes, the film touches on adventure, and rebellion. The star of *Trainspotting* and *Star Wars* leads the cast, but the exact filming location might elude many.

A. Loch Ness, Scotland
B. Glen Coe, Scotland
C. Ben Nevis, Scotland
D. D.Isle of Skye, Scotland

5. Set in the final years of the British Raj, this epic romance directed by David Lean follows a doctor as he navigates love and politics. Starring Peter O'Toole and Omar Sharif, it's often thought to have been filmed in the Middle East, but the famous desert scenes were captured in a different part of the world entirely.

A. Jordan
B. Spain
C. Morocco
D. India

6. This modern-day masterpiece directed by Martin Scorsese, featuring Leonardo DiCaprio and Matt Damon, tells the tale of a police informant in a gritty, crime-filled city. However, the exterior shots of a crucial building were not filmed in Boston, as the movie suggests, but in this European city.

A. Berlin, Germany
B. Dublin, Ireland
C. Rome, Italy
D. London, England

7. In this Terrence Malick film starring Colin Farrell and Christian Bale, the lush and dangerous backdrop of the early Americas is stunningly recreated. But the Jamestown colony wasn't filmed in Virginia; the setting for this historical tale is actually much farther south.

A. Florida, USA
B. North Carolina, USA
C. Georgia, USA
D. Costa Rica

8. Known for its wild car chases and apocalyptic desert landscapes, this recent installment of a dystopian action series directed by George Miller stars Tom Hardy and Charlize Theron. Though it seems to be set in an arid wasteland, much of it was shot in a remote corner of this country.

    A. Australia
    B. Namibia
    C. Tunisia
    D. Saudi Arabia

9. An epic journey set against towering glaciers and sweeping grasslands, this film features DiCaprio in his grittiest performance yet. Directed by Alejandro González Iñárritu, it feels like the American frontier, but most of the filming took place much farther north.

    A. Montana, USA
    B. Alberta, Canada
    C. Alaska, USA
    D. Patagonia, Argentina

10. A gripping war film directed by Mel Gibson, this story about a soldier's refusal to carry a weapon during World War II stars Andrew Garfield. The battle scenes were intense, but the rocky cliffs where much of the action was filmed were not in Okinawa, as the movie suggests.

A. Hawaii, USA

B. Queensland, Australia

C. New Zealand

D. Philippines

Answers

1. B. Oregon, USA – *The Shining*

- While *The Shining* is set in Colorado, the exterior shots of the Overlook Hotel were filmed at Timberline Lodge in Oregon, at the base of Mount Hood. The interior shots were filmed on elaborate sets in the UK.

2. C. Rosarito, Mexico – *Titanic*

- James Cameron's *Titanic* was famously filmed at a giant water tank in Rosarito, Mexico. Despite the film's icy setting, much of the filming took place in sunny, warm weather on the Pacific coast.

3. C. Sölden, Austria – *Inception*

- The snow fortress scenes in *Inception* were filmed in the ski resort of Sölden, Austria. The film's complex narrative takes audiences through layers of dreams, with the snowy sequences adding a dramatic backdrop.

4. D. Isle of Skye, Scotland – *Shallow Grave*

- *Shallow Grave* was Danny Boyle's first film, starring Ewan McGregor. Its dark humor and psychological tension are offset by the beautiful, dramatic landscapes of Scotland's Isle of Skye.

5. B. Spain – Lawrence of Arabia

- Though *Lawrence of Arabia* is set in the Middle East, much of the desert scenes were filmed in the Tabernas Desert in southern Spain. David Lean chose Spain for its vast, unspoiled landscapes.

6. B. Dublin, Ireland – *The Departed*

- While *The Departed* is set in Boston, many of the key exterior shots, including the famous rooftop scenes, were filmed in Dublin, Ireland. Scorsese often shoots outside the U.S. for budget reasons.

7. C. Georgia, USA – *The New World*

- Terrence Malick's *The New World* was set in Virginia, but many scenes were filmed in Georgia due to its lush, unspoiled landscapes, which stood in for the early American colonies.

8. B. Namibia – Mad Max: Fury Road

- *Mad Max: Fury Road* was primarily filmed in the Namib Desert in Namibia. Director George Miller chose this location for its stunning, otherworldly landscapes, which perfectly captured the dystopian feel of the film.

9. B. Alberta, Canada – *The Revenant*

- *The Revenant* was filmed in the Canadian wilderness of Alberta, where freezing temperatures and difficult terrain added to the film's realism. Leonardo DiCaprio's role earned him an Academy Award for Best Actor.

10. B. Queensland, Australia – *Hacksaw Ridge*

While *Hacksaw Ridge* is set in Okinawa, Japan, the actual filming took place in Queensland, Australia. The Australian landscape was chosen for its resemblance to the rugged, war-torn terrain of Okinawa.

Quiz 6

Famous Songs and Music Video Locations

Each question gives you cryptic clues about a famous music video's **filming location**. Use hints about the **city**, **artist**, and **song** to match the video to the correct location. Choose the correct answer from the options below.

1. "Don't Let Me Down" – The Beatles

This video captured the Fab Four performing live on a rooftop in the same city where they recorded their legendary *Abbey Road* album. It's also the city where their iconic pedestrian crossing became a symbol of rock history. Their spontaneous rooftop concert left fans below in awe.

A. London
B. Liverpool
C. Manchester
D. Birmingham

2. "Where the Streets Have No Name" – U2

This famous rooftop performance stopped traffic in a sprawling city known for its beaches and film industry. It's not where the band originates from, but it's a city synonymous with glamour and celebrities. Bono and the band almost caused a riot here.

A. London, United Kingdom
B. Los Angeles, USA
C. Dublin, Ireland
D. New York City, USA

3. "Empire State of Mind" – Jay-Z ft. Alicia Keys

This song is an ode to the city that raised Jay-Z, known for its yellow taxis.

A. Chicago, USA
B. Los Angeles, USA
C. New York City, USA
D. Miami, USA

4. "Viva La Vida" – Coldplay

Though this video features surreal imagery, the song draws inspiration from the grand cathedrals and ancient architecture of a city known for its revolutionary history and Renaissance art. The band hails from another country, but this European capital set the stage for their artistic vision.

A. Florence, Italy
B. Paris, France
C. Rome, Italy
D. London, UK

5. "Hello" – Adele

In this emotionally charged video, Adele is seen in an old countryside home, reflecting on lost love. The song was recorded in a city famous for its foggy weather, world-class theater, and a massive river that runs through its heart. Adele, a native of this city, carries its soulful vibe with her.

A. Manchester
B. Liverpool
C. Glasgow
D. London

6. "Angels" – Robbie Williams

This emotional anthem was filmed in a countryside setting just outside the city where Robbie Williams was born and raised. Known for its football culture and industrial history, this city helped shape one of Britain's most charismatic pop stars.

A. Monaco

B. Birmingham

C. Stoke-on-Trent

D. Manchester

7. Bohemian Like You – The Dandy Warhols

This iconic early 2000s indie anthem features scenes from a city known for its vibrant counterculture, quirky festivals, and its "keep weird" slogan. The band, originally from X, chose this city for its laid-back and artsy vibe, where the video was filmed.

A. Seattle

B. Portland

C. Austin

D. San Francisco

8. "Take On Me" – A-ha

This groundbreaking video, featuring animated pencil sketches, was set in a small café in this city, known for its fjords and modern Scandinavian design. A-ha, the band behind this massive 80s hit, hails from this Northern European country.

A. Copenhagen, Denmark

B. Oslo, Norway

C. Helsinki, Finland

D. Stockholm, Sweden

9. "God's Plan" – Drake

Drake's viral music video features him giving away $1 million in donations to people in a city where he is hailed as a hometown hero. Known for its hockey team and multicultural neighborhoods, this Canadian city serves as Drake's creative and personal hub.

A. Vancouver
B. Montreal
C. Toronto
D. Ottawa

10. "Wrecking Ball" – Miley Cyrus

This raw and emotional video features Miley swinging on a wrecking ball. The singer, who grew up near a city famous for its country music scene, began her career here before becoming a global pop sensation.

A. Austin, Texas
B. Los Angeles, California
C. Nashville, Tennessee
D. New Orleans, Louisiana

Answers

1. A. London – *Don't Let Me Down* (The Beatles)

- The Beatles' iconic rooftop concert, where they performed "Don't Let Me Down," took place on the rooftop of the Apple Corps building in

London in 1969. This surprise show was their last public performance as a group, drawing crowds below on the streets of London.

2. B. Los Angeles – Where the Streets Have No Name (U2)

- U2 filmed their *Where the Streets Have No Name* music video on a rooftop in downtown Los Angeles in 1987. The performance caused chaos, with police shutting down parts of the city due to the massive crowd that gathered to watch the band.

3. C. New York City – *Empire State of Mind* (Jay-Z ft. Alicia Keys)

- Jay-Z and Alicia Keys filmed *Empire State of Mind* in New York City, with scenes featuring landmarks like the Empire State Building, Times Square, and the Brooklyn Bridge. The song became an anthem for the city, celebrating its resilience and energy.

4. B. Paris – *Viva La Vida* (Coldplay)

- While the *Viva La Vida* music video features abstract imagery, Coldplay's song draws inspiration from the art and history of Paris. The title itself, which means "Live the Life," hints at themes of revolution and renewal.

5. D. London – *Hello* (Adele)

- Though Adele's *Hello* video was filmed in the Canadian countryside, her musical roots are deeply tied to London. She grew up in Tottenham and has often credited her hometown for shaping her soulful sound and storytelling style.

6. C. Stoke-on-Trent – *Angels* (Robbie Williams)

- Robbie Williams was born in Stoke-on-Trent, and this city is often referenced in his music. The song *Angels*, one of his biggest hits, is accompanied by a video filmed in a countryside estate outside of London, but the singer's heart belongs to his hometown.

7. B. Portland – *Bohemian Like You* (The Dandy Warhols)

- The Dandy Warhols are Portland natives, and the video for *Bohemian Like You* perfectly captures the quirky and eccentric atmosphere of the city. Portland is known for its indie music scene, alternative culture, and the slogan "Keep Portland Weird."

8. B. Oslo – *Take On Me* (A-ha)

- The music video for *Take On Me*, featuring a mix of live-action and pencil sketch animation, was a pioneering work in the 1980s. A-ha, the band behind this international hit, hails from Oslo, Norway.

9. C. Toronto – *God's Plan* (Drake)

- Drake filmed the viral *God's Plan* video in his hometown of Toronto, where he donated money to local residents, schools, and charities. Toronto is a major part of Drake's identity, and he frequently references the city in his music.

10. C. Nashville – *Wrecking Ball* (Miley Cyrus)

- Miley Cyrus grew up near Nashville, Tennessee, the city known as the heart of country music. Though she's now a pop icon, her early music career was rooted in Nashville's country music scene, where her father, Billy Ray Cyrus, also made his name.

Quiz 7

Festivals of the World - Celebrate Like a Local!

1. This famous Brazilian festival is known for its parades, samba dancing, and colorful costumes, and is held annually in the city of Rio de Janeiro.

A. Mardi Gras

B. Carnival

C. Oktoberfest

D. La Tomatina

2. Which Hindu festival is known as the "Festival of Lights," celebrated with fireworks, the lighting of lamps, and family gatherings?

A. Diwali

B. Holi

C. Vesak

D. Ramadan

3. Held annually in New Orleans, this festival features parades, masks, and beads, and culminates in the last day before Lent.

A. Bastille Day

B. Mardi Gras

C. Carnival

D. Cinco de Mayo

4. Which country is famous for its "Running of the Bulls" event, which is part of the San Fermin Festival?

A. Spain

B. Mexico

C. Italy

D. Portugal

5. In Munich, Germany, you can raise your stein at this world-famous beer festival held every year, featuring traditional Bavarian music, food, and, of course, beer.

A. Fasching

B. Beer Week

C. Harvest Festival

D. Oktoberfest

6. In Thailand, this festival celebrates the new year by splashing water on each other to symbolize cleansing and renewal.

A. Songkran

B. Tet

C. Loy Krathong

D. Vesak

7. The iconic "Burning Man" festival, known for its artistic and creative spirit, takes place in which U.S. desert?

    A. Mojave Desert

    B. Death Valley

    C. Black Rock Desert

    D. Sonoran Desert

8. Which festival, held annually in the city of Harbin, China, is famous for its intricate ice sculptures and freezing temperatures?

    A. Sapporo Snow Festival

    B. Ice Festival

    C. Harbin International Ice and Snow Sculpture Festival

    D. Winter Carnival

9. Known as the "largest tomato fight in the world," this festival takes place in the town of Buñol, Spain.

    A. La Tomatina

    B. Feria de Abril

    C. San Fermin

    D. Las Fallas

10. Celebrated every year in India and Nepal, this festival involves throwing brightly colored powders and marks the arrival of spring.

    A. Diwali

    B. Eid al-Fitr

C. Holi

D. Baisakhi

11. Which Scottish festival celebrates New Year's Eve with fireballs and torchlight processions in the town of Stonehaven?

A. Hogmanay

B. Beltane

C. Samhain

D. Up Helly Aa

12. Held in Switzerland, this winter festival in the town of Evolène involves locals dressing up as fearsome figures known as "Peluches" to ward off evil spirits.

A. Fasnacht

B. Fête des Vignerons

C. Carnival of Basel

D. Le Carnaval d'Evolène

13. Which Japanese festival is held annually in Kyoto and dates back over 1,000 years, featuring ancient customs, traditional costumes, and a grand parade?

A. Aoi Matsuri

B. Gion Matsuri

C. Obon

D. Tanabata

14. Known for its surreal and dreamlike experience, this festival in Spain involves participants creating and setting fire to massive effigies in the streets of Valencia.

A. Feria de Abril

B. Las Fallas

C. Semana Santa

D. San Isidro

15. What is the name of the unique Mexican holiday that honors the dead, celebrated with vibrant altars, marigold flowers, and sugar skulls?

A. Dia de los Muertos

B. Cinco de Mayo

C. Posadas

D. El Grito de Dolores

Answers

1. B. Carnival

- Rio's Carnival is the biggest in the world, attracting over 2 million people per day during the festival's peak. The samba parades are the most iconic feature of the celebration.

2. A. Diwali

- Diwali is celebrated by millions of Hindus, Jains, Sikhs, and Buddhists. It symbolizes the victory of light over darkness and good over evil.

3. B. Mardi Gras

- Mardi Gras means "Fat Tuesday" in French, referring to the practice of eating rich foods before the fasting period of Lent begins.

4. A. Spain

- The San Fermin Festival, held in Pamplona, includes the "encierro" or Running of the Bulls, where participants run ahead of a group of bulls through the city streets.

5. D. Oktoberfest

- Oktoberfest originally began in 1810 as a royal wedding celebration. Today, it attracts millions of people to Munich every year to enjoy beer, food, and festivities.

6. A. Songkran

- Songkran is celebrated every April and is known for its water fights, symbolizing the washing away of bad luck for the new year.

7. C. Black Rock Desert

- Burning Man is not just a festival—it's a temporary community that embraces self-expression, art, and sustainability in Nevada's Black Rock Desert.

8. C. Harbin International Ice and Snow Sculpture Festival

- Harbin's Ice Festival showcases intricate sculptures made entirely of ice and snow, some of which are illuminated with colorful lights.

9. A. La Tomatina

- La Tomatina began in 1945 when a spontaneous food fight broke out during a parade. Today, thousands of people gather to throw tomatoes in the streets of Buñol.

10. C. Holi

- Holi, also known as the "Festival of Colors," is celebrated with a joyous mix of dancing, singing, and throwing of vibrant powders to mark the end of winter and the triumph of good over evil.

11. A. Hogmanay

- Hogmanay is Scotland's traditional New Year's Eve celebration, and the fireball ceremony in Stonehaven is believed to ward off evil spirits for the coming year.

12. D. Le Carnaval d'Evolène

- The Carnaval d'Evolène features "Peluches," figures covered in fur and horns, who parade through the town to scare away winter's demons.

13. B. Gion Matsuri

- Gion Matsuri is Kyoto's most famous festival and dates back to 869 AD. It features a month-long celebration, with the grand procession of floats, known as *Yamaboko Junko*, as its highlight.

14. B. Las Fallas

- Las Fallas is celebrated in Valencia, where large puppets and effigies (called *ninots*) are burned in a fiery spectacle known as *La Cremà* on the festival's final night.

15. A. Dia de los Muertos

- Dia de los Muertos, or Day of the Dead, is a Mexican holiday where families honor their deceased loved ones with vibrant altars, offerings, and celebrations, believing that the spirits return to visit the living.

Quiz 7

World Leaders (Modern History Edition) - Who Am I?

In this quiz, we dive into the lives and actions of pivotal figures who have shaped the modern world. Think you know your modern history? Get ready to test your knowledge with cryptic clues that hint at some of the most influential leaders, activists, and revolutionaries. From Cold War superpowers to civil rights movements, this quiz will challenge you to think beyond the obvious.

1. I led my people through a struggle against apartheid, spending decades in prison before emerging as a global symbol of peace and reconciliation. After my release, I became the first leader of a newly united country. My name is synonymous with forgiveness.

   Who am I?

2. I was a pacifist who led a movement for independence from British rule, often fasting as a form of protest. Though my methods were peaceful, my assassination in 1948 shocked the world. Today, I'm remembered for my simple clothes and profound wisdom.

Who am I?

3. I stood at the helm during one of my nation's darkest hours, giving rousing speeches that rallied my people during the Blitz. With a cigar in hand and a fierce determination, I helped lead the Allied forces to victory in World War II.

Who am I?

4. A symbol of defiance against segregation, I made history by refusing to give up my seat on a bus in the American South. My quiet act of resistance sparked a nationwide civil rights movement. Today, I'm remembered as an icon of courage.

Who am I?

5. I was a key figure during the Cuban Missile Crisis, and my name became synonymous with the rise of communism in the Western Hemisphere. Leading my nation from the jungles to the international stage, I challenged the world's superpowers during the Cold War.

Who am I?

6. I delivered a speech from the steps of the Lincoln Memorial that echoed across America. With my words of hope and equality, I became the voice of the civil rights movement in the 1960s. Though my life was cut short, my dream lives on.

Who am I?

7. As the first female prime minister of my country, I earned the nickname "The Iron Lady" for my unwavering leadership. I oversaw economic reforms and led my nation through the Falklands War, leaving an enduring legacy.

Who am I?

8. I am the reformer who helped dismantle the Soviet Union from within. My policies of perestroika and glasnost led to increased openness and restructuring, but they also hastened the fall of my country's once-mighty empire.

Who am I?

9. I led China through a period of great change, opening the country to the world while maintaining strict control. My legacy is complex—praised for my economic reforms, but remembered for my government's violent crackdown on student protests.

Who am I?

10. I am a Nobel laureate and a beacon of human rights. Leading a movement to restore democracy in my country, I endured house arrest for over a decade. My leadership has been both celebrated and criticized in recent years.

Who am I?

Answers

1. Nelson Mandela – Former President of South Africa

- Mandela spent 27 years in prison for his activism against apartheid before becoming South Africa's first Black president in 1994. His dedication to peace and reconciliation earned him the Nobel Peace Prize in 1993, and his autobiography, *Long Walk to Freedom*, details his incredible journey.

2. Mahatma Gandhi – Leader of India's Independence Movement

- Gandhi's philosophy of nonviolent resistance, or *Satyagraha*, inspired civil rights movements across the globe. He played a key role in India's independence from British rule in 1947. Despite his peaceful approach, he was assassinated in 1948 by a nationalist who opposed his ideals of tolerance.

3. Winston Churchill – Former Prime Minister of the United Kingdom

- Churchill's leadership during World War II, especially his defiant speeches like "We shall fight on the beaches," bolstered British morale during the darkest days of the Blitz. He was awarded the Nobel Prize in Literature in 1953 for his historical writings.

4. Rosa Parks – Civil Rights Activist

- Rosa Parks' refusal to give up her seat to a white passenger in Montgomery, Alabama, in 1955 became a pivotal moment in the civil rights movement. Her quiet bravery helped ignite the Montgomery Bus Boycott, which was led by a young Martin Luther King Jr.

5. Fidel Castro – Former Leader of Cuba

- Fidel Castro came to power in 1959 after leading a revolution against Cuban dictator Fulgencio Batista. Under his leadership, Cuba became a communist state and was a central figure in the Cold War, most notably during the Cuban Missile Crisis of 1962 when the world came close to nuclear war.

6. Martin Luther King Jr. – Civil Rights Leader

- King's "I Have a Dream" speech, delivered during the March on Washington in 1963, remains one of the most famous speeches in history. He advocated for nonviolent protest and was awarded the Nobel Peace Prize in 1964. His assassination in 1968 shocked the world.

7. Margaret Thatcher – Former Prime Minister of the United Kingdom

- Thatcher became Britain's first female prime minister in 1979 and served until 1990. Her policies, known as "Thatcherism," focused on deregulation, privatization, and reducing the power of trade unions. Her role in the Falklands War cemented her reputation as a tough and decisive leader.

8. Mikhail Gorbachev – Former Leader of the Soviet Union

- Gorbachev's policies of *perestroika* (restructuring) and *glasnost* (openness) were intended to modernize the Soviet Union, but they ultimately contributed to its collapse in 1991. He received the Nobel Peace Prize in 1990 for his role in ending the Cold War.

9. Deng Xiaoping – Former Leader of China

- Deng Xiaoping led China through significant economic reforms in the 1980s, opening the country to foreign investment and market-oriented reforms. However, his legacy is clouded by the 1989 Tiananmen Square Massacre, where the government violently suppressed pro-democracy protests.

10. Aung San Suu Kyi – Myanmar's Pro-Democracy Leader

- Aung San Suu Kyi, daughter of the country's independence hero, spent nearly 15 years under house arrest for her opposition to Myanmar's military junta. She was awarded the Nobel Peace Prize in 1991. However, her international reputation has been tarnished in recent years due to her government's handling of the Rohingya crisis.

Quiz 8

Vol 1 - Capital Cities Around the World

1. Known for its futuristic skyline and harsh winters, what is the capital of Kazakhstan?

A. Almaty

B. Astana

C. Shymkent

D. Bishkek

2. Famous for its medieval architecture and sitting on the banks of the Danube River, what is the capital of Slovakia?

A. Bratislava

B. Košice

C. Vienna

D. Budapest

3. This city is nestled between the Alps and the Adriatic Sea and is known for its green spaces. What is the capital of Slovenia?

A. Maribor

B. Zagreb

C. Ljubljana

D. Trieste

4. Known for its iconic canals and world-class museums, which city is the capital of the Netherlands?

A. The Hague

B. Rotterdam

C. Amsterdam

D. Antwerp

5. This capital sits high in the Andes and is known for its dramatic views and colonial charm. What is the capital of Bolivia?

A. Sucre

B. La Paz

C. Quito

D. Cusco

6. Famous for its coffeehouses and classical music, which city is the capital of Austria?

A. Salzburg

B. Innsbruck

C. Vienna

D. Munich

7. Known for its stunning fjords and proximity to the Arctic Circle, what is the capital of Norway?

A. Bergen

B. Oslo

C. Stavanger

D. Tromsø

8. This city is home to one of the world's tallest buildings and a vibrant night market scene. What is the capital of Taiwan?

A. Kaohsiung

B. Taipei

C. Tainan

D. Taichung

9. Sitting at the crossroads of Europe and Asia, which city is the capital of Turkey?

A. Istanbul

B. Baku

C. Izmir

D. Ankara

10. Famous for its modernist architecture and built as a planned city, what is the capital of Brazil?

A. Rio de Janeiro

B. São Paulo

C. Brasília

D. Salvador

Answers

1. B) Astana

- Astana, recently renamed Nur-Sultan, is one of the world's youngest capital cities, only becoming the capital in 1997.

2. A) Bratislava

- Bratislava is the only capital city in the world that borders two countries: Austria and Hungary.

3. C) Ljubljana

- Ljubljana is one of Europe's greenest capitals, with nearly 50% of the city covered by forests.

4. C) Amsterdam

- Amsterdam's famous canals are over 100 kilometers long and are home to more bicycles than people.

5. B) La Paz

- At an altitude of roughly 3,650 meters (12,000 feet), La Paz is the highest capital city in the world.

6. C) Vienna

- Vienna is often ranked as one of the most livable cities in the world, with its rich cultural scene and history of classical music.

7. B) Oslo

- Oslo is known for its proximity to nature, with forests and hills surrounding the city, making it a perfect spot for hiking and skiing.

8. B) Taipei

- Taipei is home to the famous Taipei 101 skyscraper, which was the world's tallest building until 2010.

9. D) Ankara

- Many people mistakenly think Istanbul is Turkey's capital, but Ankara took on this role in 1923 when the Turkish Republic was founded.

10. C) Brasília

- Brasília was designed by the famous architect Oscar Niemeyer, and its layout resembles an airplane when viewed from above.

Quiz 9

Flag-tastic Frenzy True or False

Below are 15 True or False questions about the flags of countries around the world. Be careful—some of them are trickier than they seem! See how many you can get right and look for fun facts after the quiz!

True or False Questions:

1. **True or False:** The flag of Switzerland is a rectangle with a red background and a white cross in the center.
2. **True or False:** The Mexican flag has an eagle holding a snake in its talon, perched on a cactus.
3. **True or False:** The flag of the United States of America originally had 13 stars representing the 13 original colonies.
4. **True or False:** The flag of Spain features a lion and a castle as part of its coat of arms.
5. **True or False:** The flag of Mozambique includes an AK-47 assault rifle, making it the only national flag with a modern firearm.
6. **True or False:** The French flag, known as the "Tricolore," consists of three vertical stripes—blue, white, and black.

7. **True or False:** The flag of South Africa was designed after the end of apartheid and features six different colors.

8. **True or False:** The flag of Denmark is considered the oldest national flag still in use today.

9. **True or False:** The flag of Egypt has three horizontal stripes—black, white, and red—along with the country's national emblem, the golden eagle, in the center.

10. **True or False:** The flag of Russia and the flag of the Netherlands are identical in color and layout.

11. **True or False:** The flag of Lebanon features a cedar tree in the middle, which is a national symbol of the country.

12. **True or False:** The flag of Greece has nine blue and white stripes, symbolizing the nine letters of the word "Freedom" in Greek.

13. **True or False:** The flag of India features a blue wheel in the center, called the Ashoka Chakra, with 24 spokes.

14. **True or False:** The flag of Nigeria consists of green, white, and green vertical stripes, symbolizing agriculture and peace.

15. **True or False:** The flag of Bhutan features a dragon, representing the country's nickname, "The Land of the Thunder Dragon."

Did You Know?

The concept of flags dates back thousands of years, with the first known flags believed to have originated in ancient China and India around 3,000 years ago. Early flags were used primarily as military and naval symbols to help identify leaders or to rally troops in battle. One of the earliest recorded instances of flag use comes from the armies of ancient Egypt, where colored banners attached to poles were used as standards to distinguish between different divisions of soldiers.

Flags became increasingly important in ancient civilizations, especially in the Middle East and Mediterranean. The Roman Empire adopted them for military purposes, while in the medieval period, flags evolved into heraldic symbols representing noble families and kingdoms. As time went on, flags took on more formalized and standardized designs, ultimately developing into the national flags we recognize today. These early uses of flags laid the foundation for the modern practice of using them to represent nations, ideals, and identities worldwide.

1. **False** - The flag of Switzerland is one of the only square national flags. It features a white cross on a red background.
2. **True** - The Mexican flag includes an eagle devouring a snake while perched on a cactus, a symbol derived from an ancient Aztec legend.

3. **True** - The original U.S. flag had 13 stars, representing the 13 original colonies. The stars were arranged in a circle.

4. **False** - Spain's flag does feature a coat of arms, but it includes a shield with two pillars, the Pillars of Hercules, not a lion and a castle.

5. **True** - The flag of Mozambique uniquely includes an AK-47 assault rifle, symbolizing defense and vigilance.

6. **False** - The French "Tricolore" consists of blue, white, and red vertical stripes, not black. The colors represent liberty, equality, and fraternity.

7. **True** - The flag of South Africa was adopted in 1994 and includes six colors: black, yellow, green, white, blue, and red, symbolizing the country's diversity.

8. **True** - The flag of Denmark, known as the "Dannebrog," is the oldest national flag still in use, with its origin dating back to 1219.

9. **True** - Egypt's flag has three horizontal stripes in black, white, and red, with the golden eagle, representing strength and power, in the center.

10. **False** - While Russia and the Netherlands both have horizontal stripes of red, white, and blue, they are in different orders. Russia's flag is white, blue, and red from top to bottom, while the Netherlands is red, white, and blue.

11. **True** - The cedar tree is a prominent symbol on Lebanon's flag, symbolizing immortality and steadiness.

12. **False** - The nine stripes on the Greek flag represent the nine syllables in the phrase "Freedom or Death" (Eleftheria i Thanatos), a motto from the Greek War of Independence.

13. **True** - India's flag includes the Ashoka Chakra, a blue wheel with 24 spokes, symbolizing the eternal wheel of law.

14. **True** - The Nigerian flag consists of three vertical stripes—two green stripes on the sides representing agriculture, and a white stripe in the middle symbolizing peace.

15. **True** - The flag of Bhutan includes a dragon holding jewels, symbolizing the country's nickname, "The Land of the Thunder Dragon," and the wealth and protection of its people.

Quiz 10

Dictators Across Global History - Who Am I?

In this quiz, we'll dive into the lives of some of the world's most notorious dictators, known for their iron-fisted rule, sweeping changes, and ruthless control over their nations. Each question offers cryptic clues, requiring you to piece together their infamous reigns. From totalitarian regimes to military juntas, these leaders left their mark on history—though not always for the better.

1. I rose from humble beginnings to become the leader of a fascist regime that plunged Europe into chaos. My dreams of a "thousand-year empire" ended in flames, and my name has become synonymous with evil.
   Who am I?

2. My "Great Leap Forward" was a disaster, and my Cultural Revolution threw my country into chaos. I ruled with an iron fist, and though my face is still on the currency, my policies left millions dead.
   Who am I?

3. I was a mustachioed ruler of my vast nation, and under my rule, millions died in purges and famines. Known for my paranoia, I built a cult of personality and transformed my country into a global superpower by force.

Who am I?

4. I seized power in my country during a coup and created a one-man dictatorship. Though once hailed as a liberator, I turned my regime into a brutal military dictatorship, with my reign marked by fear and corruption.

Who am I?

5. I'm known for my green military uniform and my fiery speeches. My reign over a small but oil-rich nation lasted for over 40 years until a NATO-backed uprising brought me down in a brutal end.

Who am I?

6. I was an Italian dictator who styled myself after the ancient Romans, creating a fascist state and aligning with a much darker force in Europe. My aggressive expansionism came to a crashing end, and my people turned on me in the final days of World War II.

Who am I?

7. I ruled my nation with an iron fist, blending a bizarre mix of Marxism and personal cult worship. I inflicted terror on my people, with

"killing fields" and labor camps as my tools of control.

Who am I?

8. I led a military dictatorship in South America, where dissent was met with brutal repression. Thousands disappeared during my regime as I tried to stamp out opposition. Today, my name is synonymous with a reign of terror.

Who am I?

9. I ruled my nation in Eastern Europe for decades, blending a combination of strict control, censorship, and secret police. My personality cult was legendary, but it all crumbled in a violent revolution that ended my life.

Who am I?

10. I'm a leader from the Middle East who ruled my country for decades with fear, secret police, and brutality. I engaged in wars with my neighbors, gassed my own people, and lived in opulence until I was overthrown by a U.S.-led coalition.

Who am I?

Answers

1. Adolf Hitler – Leader of Nazi Germany

- Hitler's rise to power in Germany led to the outbreak of World War II and the genocide of millions during the Holocaust. His regime was responsible for some of the darkest atrocities in modern history, and his reign ended with his suicide in 1945 as Allied forces closed in on Berlin.

2. Mao Zedong – Leader of the People's Republic of China

- Mao's policies, including the "Great Leap Forward" and the "Cultural Revolution," caused widespread famine, death, and destruction across China. Despite this, he remains a controversial figure, revered by some for his role in establishing modern China but reviled for the deaths of millions under his rule.

3. Joseph Stalin – Leader of the Soviet Union

- Stalin's reign was marked by massive purges, labor camps (gulags), and forced collectivization, which led to the deaths of millions of Soviet citizens. However, he also led the USSR through World War II, solidifying its status as a superpower during the Cold War.

4. Idi Amin – Leader of Uganda

- Amin's rule from 1971 to 1979 was characterized by brutal repression, human rights abuses, and economic mismanagement. His erratic behavior and ruthless policies led to the deaths of hundreds of thousands of Ugandans.

He was eventually overthrown and lived in exile until his death.

5. Muammar Gaddafi – Leader of Libya

- Gaddafi ruled Libya for over 40 years, known for his eccentric personality, bizarre speeches, and oppressive regime. He was overthrown during the Arab Spring in 2011, with his death marking the end of one of the longest-standing dictatorships in the Middle East.

6. Benito Mussolini – Leader of Fascist Italy

- Mussolini was the founder of Italian Fascism and ruled as the country's prime minister from 1922 until his downfall in 1943. He aligned Italy with Nazi Germany during World War II but was captured and executed by Italian partisans in 1945 as the war neared its end.

7. Pol Pot – Leader of Cambodia (Khmer Rouge)

- Pol Pot's Khmer Rouge regime is responsible for the deaths of nearly two million people during the Cambodian genocide. His policies, which forced millions into labor camps, resulted in starvation, torture, and executions. The "killing fields" remain a haunting legacy of his rule.

8. Augusto Pinochet – Leader of Chile

- Pinochet seized power in a coup in 1973 and ruled Chile as a military dictator for 17 years.

His regime was notorious for human rights abuses, with thousands of political opponents killed or disappeared. Despite his repression, some credit him for economic reforms that stabilized Chile's economy.

9. Nicolae Ceaușescu – Leader of Romania

- Ceaușescu's personality cult and oppressive regime led to widespread poverty and suffering in Romania. His downfall came during the Romanian Revolution in 1989, and he was executed by firing squad on Christmas Day, marking one of the most dramatic ends to a communist dictatorship in Eastern Europe.

10. Saddam Hussein – Leader of Iraq

- Saddam ruled Iraq from 1979 to 2003 with a brutal hand, using chemical weapons against his own people (the Kurds) and leading the country through devastating wars, including the Iran-Iraq War and the Gulf War. He was captured by U.S. forces in 2003 and executed after being found guilty of crimes against humanity.

Quiz 11

Vol 2 - Capital Cities Around the World

1. This capital, located in the heart of the Middle East, is known for its ancient citadel and the Dead Sea nearby. What is the capital of Jordan?

A. Beirut

B. Amman

C. Damascus

D. Riyadh

2. Known for its beautiful coastal location and centuries of Portuguese influence, what is the capital of Angola?

A. Maputo

B. Luanda

C. Kinshasa

D. Praia

3. This South Asian capital is famed for its street food and Mughal-era architecture. What is the capital of Bangladesh?

A. Kolkata

B. Dhaka

C. Islamabad

D. Karachi

4. Known for its iconic parliament building and thermal baths, what is the capital of Hungary?

    A. Vienna

    B. Zagreb

    C. Budapest

    D. Belgrade

5. Famous for its stunning modern skyline and the Petronas Towers, what is the capital of Malaysia?

    A. Kuala Lumpur

    B. Jakarta

    C. Singapore

    D. Bangkok

6. This African capital is one of the highest in elevation, known for its cool climate and rich cultural heritage. What is the capital of Ethiopia?

    A. Nairobi

    B. Addis Ababa

    C. Kampala

    D. Lusaka

7. With its rich history and ancient temples, this Southeast Asian capital is one of the most visited cities in the world. What is the capital of Thailand?

    A. Phnom Penh

    B. Yangon

    C. Hanoi

    D. Bangkok

8. Famous for its fashion scene and stunning architecture, what is the capital of Italy?

A. Milan

B. Venice

C. Rome

D. Florence

9. This capital is located on the Atlantic coast of South America and is known for its beaches and carnival. What is the capital of Uruguay?

A. Buenos Aires

B. Montevideo

C. Asunción

D. Santiago

10. Nestled in the Pyrenees mountains, this capital is one of the smallest in Europe. What is the capital of Andorra?

A. San Marino

B. Andorra la Vella

C. Vaduz

D. Luxembourg City

Answers

1. B) Amman

- Amman is one of the oldest continuously inhabited cities in the world, with human settlements dating back to 7250 BC!

2. B) Luanda

- Luanda is often called the "Paris of Africa" due to its sophisticated culture and vibrant music scene.

3. B) Dhaka

- Dhaka is known as the "City of Mosques" with hundreds of mosques scattered throughout the city.

4. C) Budapest

- Budapest was originally two cities, Buda and Pest, which were united in 1873 to form the capital we know today.

5. A) Kuala Lumpur

- Kuala Lumpur is home to the Petronas Towers, which were the tallest buildings in the world from 1998 to 2004.

6. B) Addis Ababa

- Addis Ababa is located more than 2,300 meters (7,500 feet) above sea level, making it one of the highest capitals in Africa.

7. D) Bangkok

- Bangkok's full ceremonial name is one of the longest city names in the world, with 169 characters in Thai!

8. C) Rome

- Rome is known as the "Eternal City" and is home to Vatican City, the smallest independent state in the world.

9. B) Montevideo

- Montevideo has more than 20 kilometers of beaches, making it a hotspot for summer tourism in South America.

10. B) Andorra la Vella

- Andorra la Vella is the highest capital city in Europe, sitting at an elevation of 1,023 meters (3,356 feet).

Quiz 12

Currencies of the World

1. What is the official currency of Japan?

    A. Dollar

    B. Yuan

    C. Yen

    D. Won

2. Which currency is used in Australia?

    A. Australian Euro

    B. Australian Dollar

    C. Australian Yen

    D. Australian Pound

3. What is the name of the currency used in the United Kingdom?

    A. Euro

    B. Franc

    C. Pound Sterling

    D. Dollar

4. What is the currency of Switzerland?

    A. Euro

    B. Swiss Franc

    C. Krona

    D. Dollar

5. What currency is used in South Africa?

A. Rand

B. Dinar

C. Peso

D. Rupee

6. What is the official currency of Brazil?

A. Ruble

B. Peso

C. Dollar

D. Real

7. Which currency is used in India?

A. Peso

B. Rupee

C. Yuan

D. Yen

8. What is the currency of Canada?

A. Canadian Dollar

B. Canadian Pound

C. Canadian Euro

D. Canadian Peso

9. What is the name of the currency used in South Korea?

A. Yen

B. Won

C. Yuan

D. Baht

10. What is the official currency of Mexico?

A. Peso
B. Dollar
C. Real
D. Lira

Answers

1. C) Yen

- The Japanese Yen (JPY) was introduced in 1871 as part of the Meiji government's efforts to modernize the country's economy. The word "yen" means "round object" or "circle," reflecting the shape of the coins. The yen is the third most traded currency in the world, often seen as a safe haven in times of economic instability.

2. B) Australian Dollar

- The **Australian Dollar (AUD)** replaced the Australian pound in 1966 when Australia adopted the decimal system. Often nicknamed "the Aussie," it is one of the most widely traded currencies in the Asia-Pacific region. Australia is one of the first countries to switch to polymer banknotes, which are more durable and secure than paper notes.

3. C) Pound Sterling

- The **British Pound Sterling (GBP)** is the oldest currency still in use, dating back to around 775 AD. The term "pound" comes from the Latin word "libra," meaning weight or balance. The pound was initially based on a pound of silver, which is why the currency symbol is "£," derived from the letter "L" in "libra."

4. B) Swiss Franc

- The **Swiss Franc (CHF)** was officially introduced in 1850, following Switzerland's formation as a federal state in 1848. It is known for its stability and is often used as a reserve currency due to Switzerland's neutrality and strong financial system. The Swiss Franc is also used in Liechtenstein and is regarded as a "safe haven" currency during global uncertainties.

5. A) Rand

- The **South African Rand (ZAR)** was introduced in 1961, coinciding with South Africa's transition from a British dominion to a republic. The currency gets its name from the **Witwatersrand**, the ridge where much of South Africa's gold deposits were found. South Africa is one of the world's largest producers of gold, which contributes to the rand's global significance.

6. D) Real

- The **Brazilian Real (BRL)** was introduced in 1994 as part of the **Plano Real**, a monetary reform plan that helped stabilize the Brazilian economy after years of hyperinflation. The name "real" dates back to the colonial period when Brazil was a Portuguese colony and used the Portuguese real as its currency. Today, the real is one of the strongest currencies in Latin America.

7. B) Rupee

- The **Indian Rupee (INR)** has been in use since ancient times and was standardized under British colonial rule in 1835. The symbol for the rupee (₹) was officially adopted in 2010 and is derived from the Devanagari letter "र" and the Roman letter "R." India is one of the few countries with a long-standing tradition of issuing coins made of various metals, including copper, silver, and gold.

8. A) Canadian Dollar

- The **Canadian Dollar (CAD)** was established in 1858 to replace the Canadian pound. It is colloquially referred to as the "loonie" due to the image of a common loon on the one-dollar coin.

Canada was one of the earliest adopters of polymer banknotes, similar to Australia, which makes them more resistant to counterfeiting and wear.

8. B) Won

- The **South Korean Won (KRW)** was introduced in 1945 after Korea's liberation from Japanese rule. The name "won" comes from a Chinese character that means "round," similar to the Japanese yen and Chinese yuan. South Korea experienced rapid economic growth, known as the "Miracle on the Han River," leading to the won becoming a symbol of the country's economic resilience.

9. A) Peso

- The **Mexican Peso (MXN)** is one of the oldest currencies in the Americas, dating back to the Spanish colonization in the 16th century when it was modeled after the Spanish dollar. The peso was the first currency in the world to use the "$" symbol, which later became synonymous with the US dollar. Today, the peso is the most traded currency in Latin America and is often used as a benchmark for other regional currencies.

Iconic Hotels and Resorts - Did You Know?

1. Ritz Paris (France)

- Did you know the Ritz Paris was one of the first hotels in Europe to provide en suite bathrooms, electricity, and telephones in every room? Opened in 1898, it became a favorite of Coco Chanel, who lived there for over 30 years.

2. Burj Al Arab (Dubai, UAE)

- Did you know the Burj Al Arab, often referred to as the world's only "7-star" hotel, has a helipad that has been used for some of the world's most spectacular stunts? From tennis matches with Roger Federer to Formula 1 demos, this hotel redefines luxury and spectacle.

3. The Plaza Hotel (New York City, USA)

- Did you know The Plaza is the only hotel in New York to be designated a National Historic Landmark? Opened in 1907, it has been the backdrop for numerous films, including *Home Alone 2* and *The Great Gatsby*.

4. Hotel de Glace (Quebec, Canada)

- Did you know that the Hotel de Glace is rebuilt from scratch every winter using 500 tons of ice and 15,000 tons of snow? This ice hotel melts away each spring and is recreated with a new design each year.

5. Giraffe Manor (Nairobi, Kenya)

- Did you know that Giraffe Manor is home to a herd of endangered Rothschild giraffes, which roam freely around the hotel grounds? Guests can enjoy breakfast while giraffes poke their heads through the windows for a friendly greeting.

6. The Beverly Hills Hotel (Los Angeles, USA)

- Did you know the Beverly Hills Hotel, also known as "The Pink Palace," was built in 1912, even before the city of Beverly Hills was established? It became the favored haunt of Hollywood's biggest stars, including Marilyn Monroe and Elizabeth Taylor.

9. Marina Bay Sands (Singapore)

- Did you know that Marina Bay Sands features the world's largest rooftop infinity pool? At 57 stories high, the pool offers breathtaking views of Singapore's skyline and has become one of the most photographed hotel attractions in the world.

10. Taj Mahal Palace (Mumbai, India)

- Did you know that the Taj Mahal Palace was the first hotel in India to have electricity and an elevator when it opened in 1903? It is also where India's freedom leaders, including Mahatma Gandhi, held pivotal discussions during the independence movement.

11.Ashford Castle (Ireland)

- Did you know that Ashford Castle, built in 1228, is one of the oldest castle hotels in the world? Once owned by the Guinness family, the castle features 350 acres of woodland, a private lake, and the setting for the 1951 film *The Quiet Man*.

12 Atlantis Paradise Island (Bahamas)

- Did you know that Atlantis Paradise Island is home to the largest open-air marine habitat in the world? The resort features over 50,000 marine animals in its lagoons, including sharks, rays, and tropical fish, making it a paradise for marine lovers.

Quiz 13

Vol 3 Capital Cities Around the World

1. This capital is one of the highest cities in Africa, located in the Horn of Africa region. What is the capital of Eritrea?

   A. Asmara

   B. Djibouti City

   C. Addis Ababa

   D. Mogadishu

2. Known for its vast desert surroundings and ancient ruins, what is the capital of Mauritania?

   A. Bamako

   B. Niamey

   C. Nouakchott

   D. N'Djamena

3. This Caribbean capital is known for its rich history, colonial architecture, and a UNESCO World Heritage site in its old town. What is the capital of Cuba?

   A. Santo Domingo

   B. San Juan

   C. Havana

   D. Kingston

4. This Central Asian capital is known for its rich Silk Road history and has one of the most isolated locations in the world. What is the capital of Turkmenistan?

A. Tashkent

B. Bishkek

C. Dushanbe

D. Ashgabat

5. Located in the heart of the Caucasus, this capital is known for its ancient history and unique architectural style. What is the capital of Armenia?

A. Baku

B. Tbilisi

C. Yerevan

D. Batumi

6. This island nation's capital is known for its coral reefs and beautiful lagoons. What is the capital of Kiribati?

A. Funafuti

B. South Tarawa

C. Port Vila

D. Nuku'alofa

7. Situated in the Indian Ocean, this capital is known for its pristine beaches and is the smallest capital in Africa by population. What is the capital of Seychelles?

  A. Victoria
  B. Port Louis
  C. Moroni
  D. Male

8. Famous for its distinctive white and blue houses and the nearby site of the ancient city of Carthage, what is the capital of Tunisia?

  A. Rabat
  B. Algiers
  C. Tunis
  D. Tripoli

9. This South Pacific capital is often confused with another larger city due to their similar names. What is the capital of Fiji?

  A. Port Moresby
  B. Suva
  C. Apia
  D. Nouméa

10. Known for its British colonial history and close proximity to Mount Kilimanjaro, what is the capital of Tanzania?

  A. Nairobi

B. Dodoma

C. Dar es Salaam

D. Lusaka

Answers

1. A) Asmara

- Asmara is nicknamed "Little Rome" due to its well-preserved Italian colonial architecture, making it a unique blend of African and European styles.

2. C) Nouakchott

- Nouakchott, the largest city in Mauritania, was originally a small fishing village until it became the capital in 1960. It's known for its proximity to the Sahara Desert.

3. C) Havana

- Havana's Old Town is a UNESCO World Heritage site, famous for its colorful Spanish colonial buildings and vibrant music scene.

4. D) Ashgabat

- Ashgabat holds the Guinness World Record for the most white marble-clad buildings, making it a truly striking and surreal city in the desert.

5. C) Yerevan

- Yerevan is one of the oldest continuously inhabited cities in the world, dating back to 782 BC—older than Rome!

6. B) South Tarawa

- South Tarawa is composed of a string of islets connected by causeways, making it an unusual capital that's spread across small islands in the Pacific Ocean.

7. A) Victoria

- Victoria is the smallest capital in Africa by population, and Seychelles is known for its incredible biodiversity, with giant tortoises roaming its beaches.

8. C) Tunis

- Tunis is located near the ancient city of Carthage, which was one of the most powerful cities in the ancient Mediterranean until its destruction by the Romans.

9. B) Suva

- Suva is Fiji's political and administrative center, though many confuse it with Nadi, the more tourist-friendly city located on another island.

10. B) Dodoma

- Dodoma replaced Dar es Salaam as Tanzania's capital in 1974, though Dar es Salaam remains the largest city and main commercial hub.

Quiz 14

Wildlife and National Parks

1. Which U.S. national park is home to Old Faithful, a famous geyser that erupts regularly?

    A. Yosemite National Park

    B. Yellowstone National Park

    C. Grand Canyon National Park

    D. Glacier National Park

2. Which African national park is famous for its annual Great Migration of over 1.5 million wildebeest and hundreds of thousands of zebras?

    A. Maasai Mara National Reserve

    B. Serengeti National Park

    C. Kruger National Park

    D. Chobe National Park

3. In which national park would you find Mount Kilimanjaro, the highest peak in Africa?

    A. Serengeti National Park

    B. Amboseli National Park

    C. Kilimanjaro National Park

    D. Tarangire National Park

4. Which national park in India is renowned for being home to the endangered Bengal tiger?

    A. Ranthambore National Park

    B. Sundarbans National Park

    C. Kaziranga National Park

    D. Jim Corbett National Park

5. Which marine national park in Australia is known for its vast coral reef system, the largest in the world?

    A. Great Barrier Reef Marine Park

    B. Ningaloo Reef National Park

    C. Abel Tasman National Park

    D. Galápagos Marine Reserve

6. Which national park in Uganda is famous for its population of endangered mountain gorillas?

    A. Queen Elizabeth National Park

    B. Bwindi Impenetrable National Park

    C. Volcanoes National Park

    D. Murchison Falls National Park

7. Which U.S. national park is known for its giant sequoia trees, including the General Sherman Tree, one of the largest trees in the world?

    A. Yosemite National Park

    B. Sequoia National Park

    C. Olympic National Park

    D. Zion National Park

8. Which island in the Galápagos National Park is famous for Charles Darwin's studies that led to the theory of evolution?

    A. Isabela Island

    B. Santa Cruz Island

    C. Santiago Island

    D. Floreana Island

9. In which South American national park can you find the world's largest tropical rainforest, known for its biodiversity?

    A. Torres del Paine National Park

    B. Iguazu National Park

    C. Yasuni National Park

    D. Manu National Park

10. Which national park in New Zealand is famous for its dramatic fjords, including Milford Sound, often called the "eighth wonder of the world"?

    A. Fiordland National Park

    B. Tongariro National Park

    C. Abel Tasman National Park

    D. Mount Cook National Park

Answers

1. B) Yellowstone National Park

- **Yellowstone** is so huge, it spans across three states—Wyoming, Montana, and Idaho! It's also famous for Old Faithful, a geyser that erupts like clockwork every 90 minutes. Imagine a natural alarm clock that spews boiling water 100 feet in the air—talk about punctuality!

2. B) Serengeti National Park

- Every year, **the Serengeti** throws the ultimate road trip for over 1.5 million wildebeest, with zebras tagging along for good company. Known as the **Great Migration**, it's one of the largest animal migrations on Earth—basically nature's version of rush hour, minus the honking!

3. C) Kilimanjaro National Park

- Think you've climbed a big hill? How about **Mount Kilimanjaro**, Africa's tallest free-standing mountain at 19,341 feet! Even crazier: Kilimanjaro has glaciers at its summit—yes, glaciers!—right in the middle of Tanzania. It's like finding a snow cone in the desert.

4. A) Ranthambore National Park

- Ranthambore is the ultimate tiger hide-and-seek zone, but here's a twist—**you're trying to find them!** This Indian park is one of the best places to spot the endangered Bengal tiger, which can be as elusive as your car keys on a Monday morning.

5. A) Great Barrier Reef Marine Park

- Forget building sandcastles, **the Great Barrier Reef** has built itself into the largest living structure on the planet—so big you can see it from space! With its 1,400 miles of coral, it's basically the undersea version of a sprawling metropolis... but way prettier.

6. B) Bwindi Impenetrable National Park

- This isn't just any park, it's called **Bwindi IMPENETRABLE** for a reason! Home to half the world's mountain gorillas, you can literally trek through the jungle to hang out with our fuzzy cousins. Fun fact: They don't mind staring contests, but you might lose.

7. B) Sequoia National Park

- The trees here aren't just big, they're **ridiculously enormous**. The General Sherman Tree in **Sequoia National Park** is so massive, it could fill more than 21,000 bathtubs with its trunk alone. No wonder it's known as the largest tree by volume in the world!

8. B) Santa Cruz Island

- Darwin's playground! **Santa Cruz Island** in the Galápagos is where Charles Darwin had his *"Ah-ha!"* moment about evolution. It's also home to giant tortoises that live longer than most humans. I mean, they could have seen the Beatles live!

9. D) Manu National Park

- Manu National Park in Peru is like Mother Nature's **VIP section**—it's one of the most biodiverse places on Earth! From jaguars to tapirs to more bird species than you can count, it's like walking into the ultimate animal convention. Don't forget your binoculars.

10. A) Fiordland National Park

- Ever seen a fjord? In **Fiordland National Park**, New Zealand's jaw-dropping fjords, like Milford Sound, look like something straight out of a fantasy movie (oh wait, *Lord of the Rings* was filmed nearby). Expect sheer cliffs, stunning waterfalls, and the occasional dolphin just to remind you how small you are.

Quiz 15

Transportation Systems Around the World

Questions:

1. **True or False**: The Shinkansen, also known as the "bullet train," in Japan can reach speeds of over 400 kilometers per hour (249 miles per hour).

2. **True or False**: The London Underground, also called "the Tube," is the second oldest underground railway network in the world.

3. **True or False**: In Venice, Italy, the main form of public transportation is water buses called "vaporetti" that navigate the canals.

4. **True or False**: The Paris Métro system is the busiest subway system in the world in terms of daily ridership.

5. **True or False**: The Trans-Siberian Railway is the longest railway line in the world, stretching over 9,000 kilometers (5,600 miles).

6. **True or False**: The São Paulo Metro in Brazil is the largest subway system in the Southern Hemisphere by total length of track.

7. **True or False**: The New York City subway system operates 24 hours a day, 365 days a year.

8. **True or False**: Medellín's cable car system, known as "Metrocable," was designed to connect low-income neighborhoods in the hills to the city's metro system.

9. **True or False**: The Maglev train in Shanghai, China, is the world's fastest commercial train, capable of reaching speeds over 430 kilometers per hour (267 miles per hour).

10. **True or False**: The Hong Kong Mass Transit Railway (MTR) system is one of the most unreliable public transportation systems in the world, frequently facing delays.

11. **True or False**: The Metro in Dubai is the longest fully automated and driverless metro system in the world.

12. **True or False**: The suburban railway system in Mumbai, India, carries more passengers daily than any other railway system in the world.

13. **True or False**: The Los Angeles Metro Rail is widely known for its extensive reach and popularity as a primary mode of transportation in the city.

14. **True or False**: The Gautrain in South Africa was built to connect Johannesburg and Pretoria and also provides a direct link to OR Tambo International Airport.

15. **True or False**: The Glacier Express in Switzerland is known for its fast travel through the Swiss Alps, offering one of the quickest train journeys in Europe.

Answers:

1. **False** - The Shinkansen's top speed is around 320 kilometers per hour (199 miles per hour), not over 400 km/h.
2. **False** - The London Underground, opened in 1863, is the oldest underground railway in the world.
3. **True** - Venice uses **vaporetti** (water buses) as its primary mode of public transportation through its intricate canal system.
4. **False** - The Paris Métro, though dense, is not the busiest subway in the world. That title belongs to the Tokyo Subway system.
5. **True** - The Trans-Siberian Railway is indeed the longest railway line in the world, covering over 9,000 kilometers.
6. **False** - The **Santiago Metro** in Chile is the largest in the Southern Hemisphere, not São Paulo's.
7. **True** - The New York City subway is one of the few transit systems in the world that operates 24/7.

8. **True - Medellín's Metrocable** was created to connect the city's poor, hilly neighborhoods to its central metro, improving access to jobs and services.

9. **True** - The Maglev train in Shanghai is the fastest commercial train in the world, reaching over 430 kilometers per hour.

10. **False** - The Hong Kong MTR is renowned for its reliability, with over 99% on-time performance, making it one of the most punctual systems globally.

11. **True** - The **Dubai Metro** is the longest fully automated metro network in the world, stretching over 89 kilometers.

12. **True** - Mumbai's suburban railway system is one of the busiest in the world, carrying millions of passengers daily.

13. **False** - The Los Angeles Metro Rail is not very extensive and is less popular compared to other public transit systems due to the city's car-centric culture.

14. **True** - The **Gautrain** connects Johannesburg and Pretoria with a direct link to OR Tambo International Airport, offering a fast and efficient service.

15. **False** - The **Glacier Express** is famously slow, marketed as the "slowest express train in

the world," allowing passengers to enjoy the scenic Swiss Alps.

Quiz 16

Word Association

Welcome to the **Word Association Quiz**! In this quiz, you'll be given three specific clues that are uniquely associated with a country. Your task is to identify the country based on those three clues. But be warned—these aren't the typical, easy associations like "pasta" for Italy. Instead, you'll need to think a bit deeper about culture, geography, history, and national identity. Let's see how many you can get right!

1. Clues:

- Fado music
- Azulejos
- Douro   River wine

2. Clues:

- Sumo wrestling
- Cherry blossoms
- Capsule hotels

3. Clues:

- Saunas
- Reindeer herding
- Midnight Sun

4, Clues:

- Fjords
- Viking ships
- Northern Lights

5. Clues:

- Flamenco
- Running of the Bulls
- La   Tomatina festival

6. Clues:

- Tango
- Mate
- Pampas

7. Clues:

- Maasai people
- Great Rift Valley
- Wildebeest migration

8. Clues:

- Windmills
- Tulip fields
- Bicycles

9. Clues:

- Fjaka (state of relaxation)
- Adriatic Sea
- Game of Thrones filming location

10. Clues:

- Vodka
- Hermitage Museum
- Ballet

11. Clues:

- Bhut Jolokia (ghost pepper)
- Hornbill Festival
- Tea plantations

12. Clues:

- Barbecue
- Carnival
- Amazon Rainforest

13. Clues:

- Fjaka
- Dubrovnik
- Dalmatian Coast

14. Clues:

- K-pop
- Hanbok
- DMZ (Demilitarized Zone)

15. Clues:

- Petra
- Bedouins
- Dead Sea

16. Clues:

- Alpine skiing
- Fondue
- Red Cross headquarters

17. Clues:

- Blue Lagoon
- Geysers
- Puffins

18. Clues:

- Kangaroo
- Didgeridoo
- Great Barrier Reef

19. Clues:

- Meze (small dishes)
- Parthenon
- Olive oil

20. Clues:

- Oktoberfest
- Autobahn
- Neuschwanstein Castle

Answers:

1. Portugal

- **Did you know** the word **"Azulejos"** comes from the Arabic word for "polished stone"? The iconic blue and white tiles of Portugal were influenced by Moorish designs and are a lasting remnant of the country's Muslim heritage.

2. Japan

- **Sumo wrestlers** actually live in communal training stables, and their entire day revolves around their sport. They are also legally required to follow strict diets to maintain their enormous weight.

3. Finland

- **Saunas** are so ingrained in Finnish culture that there's one sauna for every 2.5 people in Finland! Even diplomatic discussions have been held in saunas.

4. Norway

- Norway's **Northern Lights** (Aurora Borealis) are so magical that ancient Vikings believed they were the reflections of Valkyries' armor as they escorted warriors to Valhalla.

5. Spain

- **La Tomatina**, the famous tomato-throwing festival, started as a food fight among friends in 1945. It was banned for a time, but after protests, the Spanish government brought it back. Now, it's a world-famous event.

6. Argentina

- The tango was once considered so scandalous that it was banned in some countries. It originated in the lower-class districts of Buenos Aires, but now it's danced all over the world.

7. Kenya

- During the **Great Migration**, more than 1.5 million wildebeest cross the Maasai Mara and

Serengeti plains every year, making it one of the most spectacular wildlife events in the world.

8. Netherlands

- **Bicycles** outnumber people in the Netherlands! With more than 22 million bikes and a population of around 17 million, cycling is the Dutch way of life.

9. Croatia

- Croatia's famous **Dalmatian Coast** gave its name to the Dalmatian dog breed, which originates from the region. You can still see these spotted beauties around the area!

10. Russia

- The **Hermitage Museum** is so big that it would take more than 11 years to view each of its exhibits if you spent just one minute on each one.

11. India

- The **Bhut Jolokia**, also known as ghost pepper, is so spicy that it was used by Indian farmers to protect their crops from elephants!

12. Brazil

- During **Carnival**, the entire country of Brazil goes into party mode, with cities like Rio de Janeiro hosting massive parades featuring samba dancers and floats. But did you know Carnival is also a huge economic booster, generating millions in revenue?

13. Croatia

- The popular **Game of Thrones** series used **Dubrovnik** as the filming location for King's Landing, the capital of Westeros. Fans flock to the city to see the real-life setting of their favorite show.

14. South Korea

- **K-pop** bands train for years before debuting, with strict regimens that include voice, dance, and media training. Some trainees even live in dormitories during their training years.

15. Jordan

- The ancient city of **Petra**, also called the "Rose City," was carved into pink sandstone cliffs over 2,000 years ago and was once a bustling trading hub on the Silk Road.

16. Switzerland

- **Fondue**, the famous Swiss dish of melted cheese, was originally a peasant food, made to use up hardened cheese and stale bread during the long winter months.

17. Iceland

- Iceland's **Blue Lagoon** is a man-made geothermal spa, but the water comes from natural hot springs below the earth's surface, rich in minerals like silica and sulfur.

18. Australia

- The **didgeridoo**, one of the oldest musical instruments in the world, has been played by Indigenous Australians for over 1,000 years! It's used in ceremonial rituals and can create a variety of fascinating sounds.

19. Greece

- **Olive oil** from Greece is legendary. Some of the oldest olive trees in the world, still producing olives today, are over 2,000 years old, and ancient Greeks even used olive oil as an offering to the gods.

20. Germany

- The **Autobahn** in Germany is one of the few highways in the world with sections that have no speed limit, allowing drivers to zoom at speeds over 200 km/h!

Quiz 17

Cultural Etiquettes and Traditions

True or False

1. **True or False**: In Japan, it's considered polite to leave a small amount of food on your plate at the end of a meal.
2. **True or False**: In India, it is considered rude to eat with your left hand because it is traditionally reserved for unclean tasks.
3. **True or False**: In France, greeting someone with a firm handshake is a standard practice in formal settings.
4. **True or False**: In China, giving clocks as a gift is considered bad luck, as the word for "clock" sounds like the word for "death" in Chinese.
5. **True or False**: In Italy, tipping in restaurants is expected and you should leave at least 15-20% of the bill.
6. **True or False**: In the Middle East, showing the soles of your feet or shoes to someone is seen as an insult.
7. **True or False**: In Brazil, it's considered rude to arrive on time for social gatherings as punctuality can be seen as a sign of impatience.

8. **True or False**: In Thailand, touching someone's head is considered a friendly gesture, as the head is seen as the seat of wisdom.

9. **True or False**: In Russia, giving an even number of flowers to someone is seen as good luck.

10. **True or False**: In South Korea, pouring your own drink in a social setting is considered bad manners; you should always pour for others and allow others to pour for you.

11. **True or False**: In Mexico, it is common to greet people with a kiss on the cheek, even when meeting someone for the first time.

12. **True or False**: In Kenya, it is customary to greet people by spitting on your hand before shaking hands, as it is a sign of respect in some communities.

13. **True or False**: In Switzerland, being a few minutes late for an appointment is not considered rude as long as you have a good excuse.

14. **True or False**: In the Philippines, pointing with your lips is a common non-verbal gesture used to indicate something or someone.

15. **True or False**: In Nigeria, when offering or receiving something from someone, using both hands is a sign of respect.

Answers:

1. **False** - In Japan, it is polite to finish all the food on your plate. Leaving food is seen as wasteful and disrespectful to the effort made in preparing the meal.

2. **True** - In India, the left hand is traditionally used for unclean tasks, so it is considered impolite to use it for eating or handing things to others.

3. **False** - In France, handshakes are common but not necessarily firm. They tend to be light and quick, and people often greet with cheek kisses depending on the region.

4. **True** - In Chinese culture, giving a clock as a gift is considered bad luck because the word for "clock" (钟) sounds similar to "end" (终), which can be associated with death.

5. **False** - In Italy, tipping is not customary in the same way as in the U.S. A small tip or rounding up the bill is appreciated but not expected, as service charges are often included.

6. **True** - In many Middle Eastern cultures, showing the soles of your feet or shoes is considered offensive because the feet are considered the dirtiest part of the body.

7. **True** - In Brazil, arriving fashionably late to social events is normal, and arriving right on time can be interpreted as too eager or impatient.

8. **False** - In Thailand, the head is considered the most sacred part of the body, and touching someone's head is considered disrespectful.

9. **False** - In Russia, an **even** number of flowers is typically reserved for funerals, while an **odd** number is given for celebrations or happy occasions.

10. **True** - In South Korea, it is customary to pour drinks for others, and letting someone pour their own drink is seen as bad manners. This reflects the importance of communal behavior.

11. **True** - In Mexico, it is common to greet someone with a kiss on the cheek, even if it's the first time meeting. This is a sign of friendliness and warmth.

12. **True** - Among the Maasai people in Kenya, spitting is used as a form of greeting and blessing. For example, elders might spit on newborns to give them protection and good fortune.

13. **False** - In Switzerland, punctuality is highly valued, and being even a few minutes late is considered disrespectful. It's always best to be on time or early.

14. **True** - In the Philippines, pointing with your lips is a common non-verbal gesture, often used to subtly direct attention without using fingers.

15. **True** - In Nigeria and many other African cultures, offering or receiving something with both hands is a sign of respect and politeness.

Quiz 18

Country Themed Riddles

1. I'm a country where you can watch the sun rise over ancient temples, but if you're in the wrong place, you might find yourself running from a bull.
   What country am I?

2. I'm known for my delicious pastries, a tower that stands tall in the city of lights, and if you say "bonjour" here, you'll fit right in.
   Where am I?

3. I'm a country where you can hike to the roof of Africa, and if you like coffee, you're in the right place because it's said to have been discovered here.
   Where am I?

4. With a thousand islands, I stretch across the equator. Some think I'm just a place for beaches, but I've got a city that's sinking faster than Venice.
   Where am I?

5. My land is home to both koalas and kangaroos, but you'll find no wild tigers here. If you want to snorkel in the world's largest reef, I'm the country you'll want to visit.

Where am I?

6. I'm a land of castles and kilted dancers, where you might catch a glimpse of a mythical monster in my most famous lake.

What country am I?

7. I have mountains that touch the sky, and you'll need to be prepared to sip on mate if you visit me. I'm famous for my tango and beef, but watch out for the pampas winds!

What country am I?

8. I'm the world's biggest country, but don't let that fool you—my winters can make you feel pretty small. I've got ballet, vodka, and a square named after a color.

Where am I?

9. I'm where you'll find temples and tea, and a massive wall that stretches for miles. If you love pandas, you're in luck because they call me home.

What country am I?

10. I'm a land where you can drink from a natural spring, dive into a blue lagoon, and see the Northern Lights in all their glory. I might be cold, but I'm also one of the hottest spots for volcanoes!

Where am I?

11. I'm a country where curry is king, and vibrant festivals light up the streets. You'll find tigers,

temples, and a famous river that's said to cleanse the soul.

What country am I?

12. If you visit my land, you'll find tulips and windmills in spring, and you'll need a bike to get around. You'll also see more canals than Venice, but my people love to keep things flat.

What country am I?

13. I'm a place known for samba and Carnival, but if you go too deep into my forests, you'll meet creatures found nowhere else. I've got one of the world's biggest rainforests and a famous statue watching over my city.

Where am I?

14. Here you'll find fjords carved by glaciers, and if you wait long enough, the sky might dance for you in shades of green. Vikings once called this land home, and the seafood here is as fresh as it gets.

What country am I?

15. I'm famous for a tower that leans but hasn't fallen, and for giving the world pizza and opera. If you come here, be sure to make a wish by tossing a coin into one of my many fountains.

Where am I?

Answers:

1. **Spain** (bullfighting and temples refer to Spain's mix of ancient history and the Running of the Bulls in Pamplona)
2. **France** (the Eiffel Tower, pastries, and greeting with "bonjour")
3. **Ethiopia** (home to the origin of coffee and Mount Kilimanjaro's neighbor)
4. **Indonesia** (thousands of islands, with Jakarta sinking)
5. **Australia** (koalas, kangaroos, and the Great Barrier Reef)
6. **Scotland** (castles, kilts, and Loch Ness)
7. **Argentina** (tango, mate, pampas winds, and famous beef)
8. **Russia** (largest country, harsh winters, vodka, and Red Square)
9. **China** (Great Wall, pandas, tea, and temples)
10. **Iceland** (hot springs, volcanoes, and Northern Lights)
11. **India** (curry, tigers, festivals, and the Ganges River)
12. **Netherlands** (tulips, windmills, bikes, and canals)
13. **Brazil** (samba, Carnival, Amazon Rainforest, and Christ the Redeemer statue)
14. **Norway** (fjords, Northern Lights, and Viking history)

15. **Italy** (Leaning Tower of Pisa, pizza, and famous fountains like the Trevi Fountain)

Quiz 19

Film Locations Around the Globe – Volume 2

1. In this classic Spielberg adventure, a fearless archaeologist dodges traps in ancient temples and races Nazis to recover a legendary religious artifact. Although the movie is set in multiple locations, the iconic opening scene where a giant boulder rolls wasn't filmed in South America as you might think.

    A. Hawaii, USA

    B. Tunisia

    C. Morocco

    D. Peru

2. In this psychological thriller, a woman slowly uncovers terrifying secrets about her family while staying at a mysterious mansion. Though set in England, many of the exterior shots were filmed at a famous Gothic mansion in this country, known for its castles and misty landscapes.

    A. Scotland

    B. Ireland

    C. Wales

    D. Czech Republic

3. A superhero epic directed by Christopher Nolan, this film features a masked vigilante battling a criminal mastermind. One of the film's most thrilling action sequences, where a plane is hijacked mid-air, wasn't shot in Gotham but in a remote part of this Scandinavian country.

    A. Norway
    B. Finland
    C. Sweden
    D. Iceland

4. A visually stunning sci-fi epic, this Denis Villeneuve film takes viewers to a barren desert planet where noble houses vie for control. The vast sand dunes weren't located on another planet, but in this real-world location known for its striking landscapes.

    A. Egypt
    B. Jordan
    C. United Arab Emirates
    D. Hungary

5. This whimsical film from Wes Anderson features a pink hotel in the middle of a fictional European republic. However, the elaborate sets and exterior shots were not filmed in a made-up world but in a picturesque town in this real-life country.

    A. Poland
    B. Austria

C. Germany

D. Czech Republic

6. In this World War I epic directed by Sam Mendes, two British soldiers are sent on a harrowing mission across no man's land. The movie's intense long takes were filmed in this scenic English county, known for its rolling hills and history.

A. Kent, England

B. Salisbury Plain, England

C. Yorkshire, England

D. Somerset, England

7. A post-apocalyptic thriller starring Will Smith, this film shows a scientist trying to survive in an abandoned city infested with dark creatures. While the film appears to take place in a deserted New York, many scenes were actually filmed on location in this country.

A. Canada

B. Argentina

C. USA

D. Brazil

8. In this Tarantino historical drama, a group of Jewish soldiers plot to assassinate Nazi leaders during World War II. While set in France, a key underground bar scene was filmed in this neighboring country, known for its old-world architecture.

A. Germany
B. Czech Republic
C. C.Austria
D. Poland

9. A coming-of-age story set in the 1980s, this film by Luca Guadagnino revolves around a blossoming romance in the picturesque countryside. While set in Italy, many of the film's outdoor scenes were shot in this specific region, known for its vineyards and historic towns.

A. Tuscany, Italy
B. Veneto, Italy
C. Sicily, Italy
D. Lombardy, Italy

10. In this Danny Boyle-directed film, a young traveler stumbles upon a secret island paradise, only to discover that paradise comes with a dark side. Starring Leonardo DiCaprio, the movie was filmed on a pristine beach in a country known for its stunning islands and turquoise waters.

A. Fiji
B. Thailand
C. Indonesia
D. Philippines

Answers:

1. A. Hawaii, USA – Raiders of the Lost Ark

- The famous opening scene of *Raiders of the Lost Ark*, where Indiana Jones escapes a rolling boulder, was filmed in the tropical jungles of Hawaii, not in South America.

2. B. Ireland – The Others

- Though *The Others* is set in England, many of the exterior shots were filmed in Ireland, where the haunting landscapes perfectly matched the film's eerie tone.

3. A. Norway – The Dark Knight Rises

- The plane hijacking scene from *The Dark Knight Rises* was filmed over the snow-covered landscapes of Norway, creating a dramatic backdrop for the film's opening action sequence.

4. C. United Arab Emirates – Dune

- The desert planet of Arrakis in *Dune* was filmed in the stunning desert landscapes of the United Arab Emirates, particularly in the Liwa Desert.

5. D. Czech Republic – The Grand Budapest Hotel

- The pink, picturesque hotel in *The Grand Budapest Hotel* was actually filmed in Görlitz, a town on the German-Polish border, but many sets were constructed in the Czech Republic.

6. C. Yorkshire, England – 1917

- Much of *1917* was filmed in the rolling hills and open landscapes of Yorkshire, England, adding to the film's intense portrayal of World War I trench warfare.

7. C. USA – I Am Legend

- Despite the desolate look of New York City in *I Am Legend*, the movie was actually filmed on location in the heart of Manhattan, with large sections of the city closed off for filming.

8. A. Germany – Inglourious Basterds

- The tense underground bar scene in *Inglourious Basterds* was filmed in Germany, specifically in a historic beer cellar that added authenticity to the WWII setting.

9. D. Lombardy, Italy – Call Me by Your Name

- The romantic Italian countryside in *Call Me by Your Name* was filmed in the Lombardy region of Italy, with its lush landscapes and charming villages playing a key role in the film.

10. B. Thailand – The Beach

- *The Beach*, starring Leonardo DiCaprio, was famously filmed on the stunning Maya Bay on Koh Phi Phi Leh, an island in Thailand. Known for its crystal-clear waters and towering limestone cliffs, the location became world-famous after the movie's release and has since drawn visitors from all over the globe. However, due to the influx of tourists, the beach was temporarily closed to allow for environmental recovery.

Quiz 20

USA States Quiz

Match each state to the clue. Use the cryptic hints to help you identify which state is being described.

Choose from the states listed below:

A. California

B. Texas

C. New York

D. Florida

E. Louisiana

F. Hawaii

G. Colorado

H. Illinois

I. Alaska

J. Nevada

Questions:

1. This state is home to a giant mouse who welcomes millions of visitors each year. It also boasts warm weather and plenty of oranges. Think of a peninsula and a magical kingdom.
   Which state is this?

2. Known for its Cajun and Creole culture, this state is famous for its lively Mardi Gras

celebration, colorful parades, and spicy cuisine. A French influence is strong here, and jazz music fills the streets.

Which state is this?

3. The state that houses Hollywood, beautiful beaches, and a famous Golden Bridge. It's also home to towering redwood trees and Silicon Valley. It's the land of dreams and tech giants, stretching from sunny coasts to snowy mountains.

Which state is this?

4. This state is synonymous with wide-open spaces, cowboys, and barbecue. It's also known for oil fields and a famous city where "everything is bigger." A lone star is a symbol of pride here.

Which state is this?

5. The Windy City lies here, known for its deep-dish pizza, towering skyscrapers, and a lake that looks like an ocean. Al Capone and a giant metal bean share a history in this state.

Which state is this?

6. This tropical state is the only one made up entirely of islands. It's known for luaus, volcanoes, and surfing. Aloha is the way to greet people in this Pacific paradise.

Which state is this?

7. Known for its glittering casinos, this state is synonymous with entertainment and bright lights. It also has a famous desert where many flock to try their luck. What happens here, stays here.

Which state is this?

8. Known for its ski resorts, breathtaking Rocky Mountains, and mile-high capital, this state is a haven for outdoor enthusiasts. You'll find snow, peaks, and a healthy dose of adventure here.

Which state is this?

9. Known for its immense size and cold weather, this state has vast wilderness and is home to the northernmost point in the United States. The sun doesn't set for part of the year, and you might catch the Northern Lights.

Which state is this?

10. This state is home to a concrete jungle where dreams are made, and a world-famous statue welcomes visitors. It also boasts Broadway and some of the best bagels. The city that never sleeps is here.

Which state is this?

Answers - USA States Quiz

1. D. Florida – Disney World and oranges

- Florida is famous for Disney World in Orlando and its warm climate, ideal for growing oranges.

2. E. Louisiana – Mardi Gras and Creole cuisine

- Louisiana is known for its Mardi Gras celebrations in New Orleans, rich Creole and Cajun cuisine, and its deep French influence.

3. A. California – Hollywood, Golden Gate Bridge, and Silicon Valley

- California is home to Hollywood, the tech industry in Silicon Valley, and landmarks like the Golden Gate Bridge and redwood forests.

4. B. Texas – Cowboys, barbecue, and the Lone Star State

- Texas is renowned for its cowboy culture, barbecue, oil fields, and the saying that "everything is bigger in Texas."

5. H. Illinois – Chicago, deep-dish pizza, and Lake Michigan

- Illinois is home to Chicago, known for its deep-dish pizza, skyscrapers like the Willis Tower, and Lake Michigan.

6. F. Hawaii – Luaus, surfing, and volcanoes

- Hawaii is famous for its tropical islands, welcoming "Aloha" culture, luaus, and active volcanoes.

7. J. Nevada – Las Vegas and casinos

- Nevada is home to Las Vegas, known for its casinos, entertainment, and the slogan "What happens in Vegas, stays in Vegas."

8. G. Colorado – Rocky Mountains and ski resorts

- Colorado is known for its stunning Rocky Mountains, ski resorts, and the Mile-High City, Denver.

9. I. Alaska – Northern Lights and vast wilderness

- Alaska is known for its cold climate, vast wilderness, and being home to the northernmost point of the U.S. It also offers views of the Northern Lights.

10. C. New York – Statue of Liberty, Broadway, and the Big Apple

- New York is famous for New York City, home to the Statue of Liberty, Broadway shows, and the city that never sleeps.

Cities by the Sea - Did You Know?

Venice, Italy

Did you know that Venice is sinking? This iconic city is built on wooden stilts driven into the mud of the Venetian lagoon, and over time, the city has been slowly sinking. The crazy part? The wood has survived for centuries because it's underwater—where there's no oxygen, it doesn't rot! But with rising sea levels, Venice is fighting to stay afloat. Think of it as the city that's dancing with disaster, but in style.

Rio de Janeiro, Brazil

Did you know that **Rio** was once the capital of the Portuguese Empire? In 1808, when Napoleon invaded Portugal, the royal family packed their bags and moved their entire court to Rio! So for a while, Rio wasn't just a tropical paradise with stunning beaches—it was the heart of European royalty. Imagine an empire run from the shores of Copacabana!

San Francisco, USA

Did you know that San Francisco's famous Golden Gate Bridge wasn't always so "golden"? It was almost painted in black and yellow stripes for visibility (like a giant bumblebee) to prevent ships from hitting it! Thankfully, cooler heads prevailed, and they went with the iconic "International Orange" we know today. The city may be famous for fog, but its bridge makes sure to stand out.

Cape Town, South Africa

Did you know Cape Town was a crucial stop for ships during the Age of Exploration? This "Tavern of the Seas" was a refueling station for sailors making the long voyage from Europe to Asia. Today, it's still an international melting pot, but now people stop for world-class wines and jaw-dropping views of Table Mountain—not just provisions and a barrel of rum.

Sydney, Australia

Did you know that Sydney's famous Opera House almost didn't happen? The original architect, Jørn Utzon, left the project halfway through after a disagreement with the government. For a while, it looked like the Opera House would remain an unfinished dream. But after Utzon left, the building's construction continued, and it became one of the most recognizable structures on the planet. It's like a giant seashell sitting by the water, and boy, does it know how to steal the show!

Istanbul, Turkey

Did you know Istanbul is the only city in the world that straddles two continents—Europe and Asia? Talk about being in two places at once! Its strategic position by the Bosporus made it a historical hot spot for traders, conquerors, and emperors. From Byzantium to

Constantinople to Istanbul, this city has changed names more often than a pop star on a rebranding spree!

Dubai, UAE

Did you know that 50 years ago, Dubai was mostly desert? This shimmering metropolis on the Persian Gulf rose from the sand to become one of the most futuristic cities on Earth. They even built artificial islands shaped like palm trees and a world map! It's a place where they don't just move mountains—they build islands for fun.

Copenhagen, Denmark

Did you know Copenhagen's famous Little Mermaid statue has been decapitated **twice**? This iconic seaside statue, based on Hans Christian Andersen's tale, has had a rough go of it over the years. Despite its serene location, it's been vandalized multiple times. But like the resilient city it represents, the statue always gets put back together—no fairy godmother needed!

Lisbon, Portugal

Did you know that Lisbon was nearly wiped off the map in 1755 by one of the deadliest earthquakes in history? It triggered a tsunami and massive fires, leaving the city in ruins. But Lisbon rose from the ashes (literally), rebuilding itself into the beautiful coastal city it is today. The crazy part? It's still one of Europe's most laid-back cities—no stress, just history.

Miami, USA

Did you know Miami was founded by a woman? Julia Tuttle, often called "the Mother of Miami," convinced a railroad tycoon to extend his line to the city, essentially creating modern Miami. Today, it's one of the world's most glamorous beach cities, but its history started with orange groves, a vision, and a whole lot of determination—way before South Beach became the place to party.

Quiz 21

National Sayings Quiz

Match each country to the cryptic clue about one of its national sayings. Use the hints to help you identify which country is being described.

A. Japan
B. China
C. India
D. Russia
E. Brazil
F. Ireland
G. France
H. South Korea
I. Mexico
J. Italy

1. In this country, patience is often taught with the saying, "Fall seven times, stand up eight." It's a reminder to persevere through adversity, much like their people have in the face of natural disasters and cultural changes.
   Which country is this?

2. Here, they say, "The wind does not break a tree that bends," encouraging adaptability and

flexibility. This ancient wisdom comes from a culture deeply rooted in Taoist philosophy and harmony with nature.

Which country is this?

3. The phrase, "Don't count your chickens before they hatch," is a popular saying here, warning against celebrating victory too soon. In this vast country, known for its extremes in weather and history, nothing is certain until it happens.

Which country is this?

4. A saying from this land warns, "After the storm, the sun will shine." It's a reflection of the hopeful spirit of the people, who live in a region known for its love of carnival, samba, and football despite challenges.

Which country is this?

5. "The hen sees the snake's feet and the snake sees the hen's breast" is a cryptic saying from this country, often used to explain that each person has their own perspective, but not always the full truth.

Which country is this?

6. In this nation, known for its emphasis on community and family, you'll hear the expression, "The more you share, the more you have." It fits with their culture of hospitality and long nights of song and dance.

Which country is this?

7. This country uses the proverb, "You can't clap with one hand," to remind people that cooperation is key to success. Known for its large population and diverse cultures, it's a place where unity is often celebrated.

Which country is this?

8. In a country famous for its art, wine, and philosophy, they often say, "To live without loving is to not really live." The phrase reflects the importance of passion, beauty, and love in all aspects of life.

Which country is this?

9. "A person who removes a mountain begins by carrying away small stones" is a proverb from this country. It reflects their patient, hard-working approach to life, where small efforts are believed to lead to great success.

Which country is this?

10. In this country known for its cuisine and flair, they say, "The appetite comes with eating." It's a metaphor for how desire and ambition grow as you work toward your goals—though it also applies to their love of food.

Which country is this?

Answers

1. A. Japan – "Fall seven times, stand up eight."

- This famous Japanese proverb teaches resilience and perseverance, values deeply ingrained in Japanese culture through their history of rebuilding after natural disasters and hardship.

2. B. China – "The wind does not break a tree that bends."

- This Chinese saying reflects the importance of being adaptable and harmonious with one's surroundings, an idea central to Taoism and ancient Chinese philosophy.

3. D. Russia – "Don't count your chickens before they hatch."

- This common Russian proverb is used to warn against premature optimism. It fits with Russia's history of uncertain and often tumultuous times.

4. E. Brazil – "After the storm, the sun will shine."

- Brazilian people have a hopeful and positive outlook, which is embodied in this proverb. Despite challenges, they look forward to brighter days, just as carnival brings joy after tough times.

5. I. Mexico – "The hen sees the snake's feet and the snake sees the hen's breast."

- This Mexican proverb illustrates that everyone sees situations from their own perspective, but nobody ever sees the whole truth.

6. F. Ireland – "The more you share, the more you have."

- This Irish saying reflects their culture of generosity, hospitality, and a strong sense of community. Ireland is known for its love of song, dance, and storytelling.

7. C. India – "You can't clap with one hand."

- This Indian proverb highlights the importance of cooperation and working together. In such a large, diverse country, unity is seen as essential for success.

8. G. France – "To live without loving is to not really live."

- This French saying embodies the French passion for life, love, art, and beauty. France is famous for its romantic outlook on life.

9. B. China – "A person who removes a mountain begins by carrying away small stones."

- This Chinese proverb speaks to the value of patience and persistence, traits that are highly valued in Chinese culture.

10. J. Italy – "The appetite comes with eating."

- This Italian saying reflects both the love of good food and the idea that desires and ambitions grow as you pursue them. Italy is famous for its zest for life and love of food.

Thank You

Thank you for joining us on this adventure through the *World Explorer's Quiz Book*! We hope it has inspired you to learn more about the world's wonders, cultures, and history. As an independent publishing company, your support means the world to us. If you enjoyed the book, we'd greatly appreciate it if you could take a moment to leave a review on Amazon. Your feedback helps us continue creating fun and engaging content for curious minds like yours.

And as a thank you, scan the QR code below to unlock even more trivia and quizzes—on us! Safe travels, and we hope to see you again on your next exploration!

Printed in Great Britain
by Amazon

52521476R00089